Treating Substance Use Disorders Using Motivational Interviewing, Cognitive Behavioral Therapy, and the Stages of Change Model

Other Books in This Series

Crisis Intervention for Community Behavioral Health Service Providers in Ohio

Overcoming Reluctance in Therapeutic Relationships

Psychotherapy for Families

School-Based Mental Health Interventions Using Cognitive Behavioral Therapy Plus

Therapeutic Behavioral Services Using Interventions Based on Principles and Techniques of Cognitive Behavioral Therapy

Treating Attention Deficit Hyperactivity Disorder, Impulsivity, and Disruptive Behaviors in Children Using Behavioral Skill Building and Cognitive Behavioral Therapy Skills and Interventions

Treating Anxiety Using Cognitive Behavioral Therapy Skills and Interventions

Treating Depression Using Cognitive Behavioral Therapy Skills and Interventions

Treating Posttraumatic Stress Disorder Using Cognitive Behavioral Therapy Skills and Interventions

Treating Substance Use Disorders Using Motivational Interviewing, Cognitive Behavioral Therapy, and the Stages of Change Model

TREATMENT AND INTERVENTION MANUAL

Reinhild Boehme, LISW-S

Benjamin Kearney, PhD, *series editor*

THE INSTITUTE OF
FAMILY & COMMUNITY IMPACT

An OhioGuidestone Company
Berea, Ohio

The Institute of Family and Community Impact
An OhioGuidestone Company
www.OhioGuidestone.org

ISBN 978-1-951211-01-1
Printed in the United States of America

Contents

Preface

For mental health professionals, building trusting relationships with clients and knowing which interventions will most benefit them are challenging enough. Helping clients who are also dealing at the same time with chronic conditions such as poverty, violence, and addiction can seem overwhelming. That's especially true for behavioral health service providers who have limited experience. That's why we at OhioGuidestone have developed this series of clinical manuals to help professionals develop their skills while providing effective treatment.

OhioGuidestone, the largest community behavioral health organization in Ohio, regularly trains new therapists and other behavioral health interventionists to work with clients who face severe, therapy-interfering challenges. We've brought that experience to these manuals.

In this era of managed care oversight, tight funding, and pressure to deliver evidence-based or informed care, it is essential for new therapists to get up to speed on best practices quickly. It is also essential for experienced clinicians to be well provided with effective and varied treatment plans. The manuals in this series provide step-by-step guidance on evidence-based and informed treatment modalities and interventions that can be used by both licensed and unlicensed mental health professionals—as well as by their supervisors for training purposes.

Seasoned mental health professionals will find the resources offered in these manuals useful for developing a renewed focus on evidence- and research-based interventions. At OhioGuidestone, our interventions are grounded in cognitive behavioral science and also shaped by the relational and attachment scientific advances that continue to inform the behavioral health field (especially the interpersonal neurobiology work published by W. W. Norton & Company). We understand the demands of serving client populations experiencing trauma and toxic stress. Our interventions are designed not to address discrete diagnoses (clients often have more than one) but rather the symptoms that are related to them. The series addresses a wide range of issues, such as depression, anxiety, ADHD, PTSD, and even reluctance to engage in therapy, and it provides interventions for children and adults.

We cannot "fix" our clients. But we can guide them along clear paths toward developing the skills they need to navigate the challenges they face, in their thoughts and in their lives. It's our sincere hope that the books in this series will help better prepare more mental health professionals to do just that.

— Benjamin Kearney, PhD, series editor

If you purchased this manual and want to make copies of interventions to help your clients, please do so. However, please do not share copies with other professionals but encourage them to buy manuals for themselves. This will help us continue to add to and update this series, to better equip all helpers who make a difference.

Acknowledgments

Thanks to Lynn Franks, Jason Goldswer, Jeff Howell, Haley McFarland, and Katherine Mullin for lending their time, creativity, and enthusiasm. I could not have had a better team!

Introduction

Why can it be so difficult to provide effective treatment for substance use disorders (SUDs)? As integrated treatment of substance use disorders and mental health conditions is rapidly becoming the standard of care, how are the fields of mental health and addiction treatment merging their theoretical bases? What does this merging of fields look like in practice?

This intervention manual is for licensed and nonlicensed professionals who provide addiction treatment. You will find interventions that are designed to meet your clients where they are—and to cater the treatment approach used to where they are.

There are at least three pillars of addiction treatment we will briefly review in this introduction. They are:

- The Stages of Change Model (Prochaska, Redding, & Evers, 2008)

- Motivational Interviewing and Counseling (Miller and Rollnik, 2013)

- Cognitive Behavioral Therapy (Beck, 2011)

Additionally, all treatment, be it for mental health conditions or SUDs, takes place under the roof of empathic connection. No treatment modality or technique will be effective if the treatment provider is not meaningfully and empathically connected with their client, willing to listen to and feel with their client in order to better understand their client's world and experience. Empathy is always the starting point. Without empathy, treatment never really begins. Empathy says: "I see you and your pain. I accept who you are. I take your experiences and your world seriously. I am here to listen. I am here for you."

Some interventions in this manual include an integrated spiritual element or an optional spiritual component. These are indicated with a heart symbol ♥ next to the intervention title. For the purpose of this manual, spirituality is defined as any connection with a higher power or purpose that contributes to a sense of safety, meaning, community, and connection with self, others, and the world.

Stages of Change

The Stages of Change Model provides a roadmap for addiction treatment. Depending on where and how the model is applied, the number and names of stages may vary. For this manual we will outline interventions based on the following stages of change:

- Precontemplation
- Contemplation
- Preparation
- Action
- Maintenance
- Relapse Prevention

It's best to think of the stages of change as flexible and nonlinear. A linear model would assume that your client will neatly move through each stage. In reality, clients in recovery move between stages often. A relapse may send your client back into the precontemplation or contemplation stage. This does not mean that there is anything wrong with your client or the treatment. Nonlinear progression is a part of SUD treatment. Of course, the goal is to help your client move toward and reach the maintenance stage. The path to this goal, however, can be short and straight or long and winding.

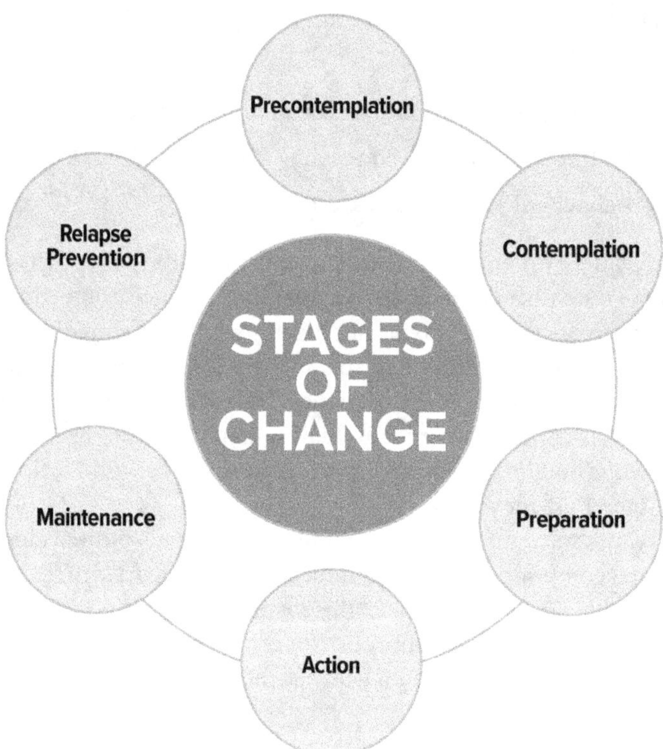

Figure 1

Think of each stage of change as a moving part. When there is a relapse, your client may visit the contemplation stage again. During the action stage, it's a good idea to visit the relapse prevention stage and so forth. It's also possible, though rare, that your client arrives in treatment ready for the action stage of treatment. When this happens, it's important to recognize this and meet your client where she is.

Prochaska and Norcross (2001) warn against "treating all patients as though they are in action." Assuming clients are ready, willing, and able to become sober when they are are not is detrimental to treatment. Accurate assessment of your client's present stage of change is imperative.

Here is a simple way to think about each stage of change:

Precontemplation	"There is nothing wrong with me. I have no idea why you are bothering me."
Contemplation	"I am wondering if I should make some changes to my drinking/drug use."
Preparation	"I need to make some changes and am getting ready to do so."
Action	"I am working on my sobriety and recovery."
Maintenance	"I am sober and in recovery. I take daily steps to keep it that way."
Relapse Prevention	"I understand that relapse is often part of addiction. I have a relapse prevention plan."

Motivational Interviewing

As a general rule, the earlier stages of change (precontemplation, contemplation, and preparation) call for the use of motivational interviewing (MI). This is because your client has not yet decided or isn't quite ready to become sober and work on recovery. MI calls for the use of open-ended questions that help clients clarify tension between the life they are living and the life they want, and perhaps tension between the life they are living and their values. Over time, your clients can then move toward the change they want. Of course, MI can still be used in later stages of treatment.

Motivational interviewing acknowledges that no treatment provider can make a client change. Rather, it is the client's decision to make the changes he can and wants to make. When you are using MI, you are helping your client access his internal compass. Perhaps he has not paid attention to this compass for quite some time. Your open-ended questions are helping your client pause and think about what he wants and needs and how he can get those things.

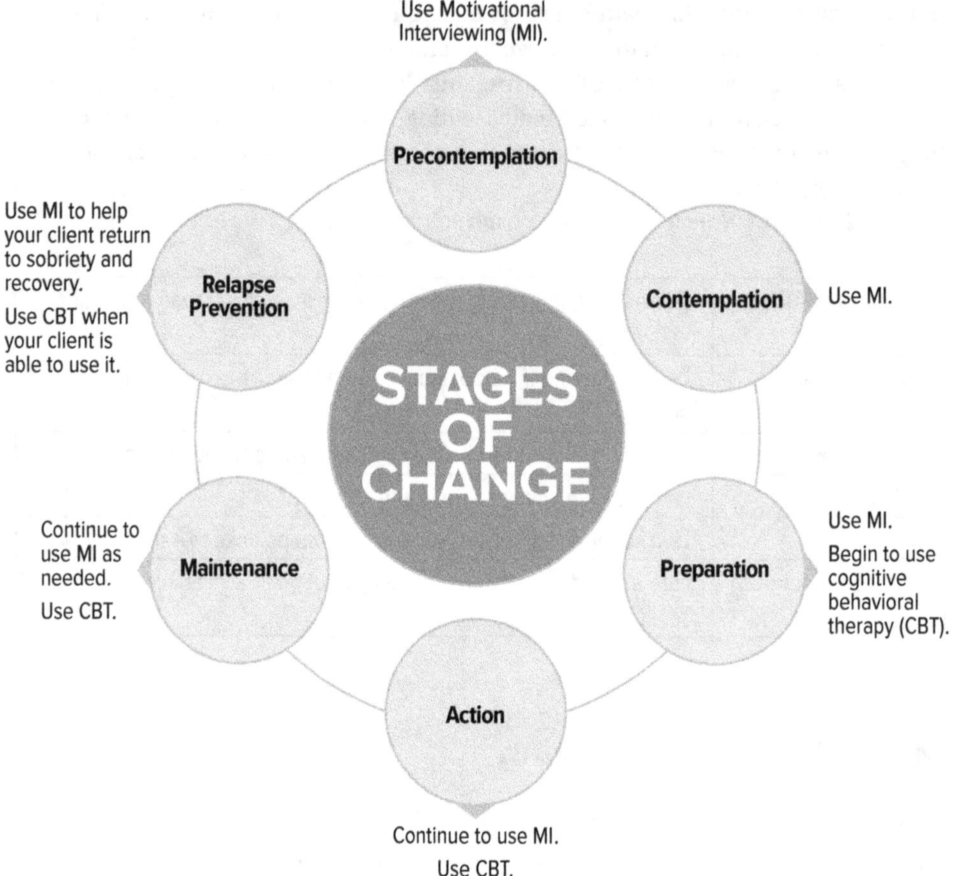

Figure 2

For a quick introduction to MI you may want to read:

Skinner, W., Cooper, C., Chamberlain, C., Ravitz, P., & Maunder, R. (2013). *Motivational interviewing for concurrent disorders*. New York: W. W. Norton.

For a more in-depth introduction, read:

Miller, W. R., & Rollnick, S. (2013). *Motivational interviewing: Helping people change*. New York: Guilford Press.

Cognitive Behavioral Therapy (CBT)

CBT will help your clients learn to examine and change the way they think, act, and feel. Specifically, your client will learn to examine thinking, feelings, and behaviors that contribute to maintaining addiction verses thinking, feelings, and behaviors that enhance sobriety and recovery. For further information about CBT, you may want to read:

Boehme, R. (2018). *Treating Anxiety: Using Cognitive Behavioral Therapy Skills and Interventions*. Berea, OH: The Institute for Family and Community Impact.

For an in-depth introduction to CBT you can read:

Tolin, D. F. (2016). *Doing CBT: A comprehensive guide to working with behaviors, thoughts, and emotions.* New York: Guilford Press.

Keep in mind that you can't use CBT until your client has made at least a tentative commitment to change and is willing to examine his thinking, feeling, and behavior.

Interventions

Psychotherapy Interventions

The following interventions are designed to be provided by licensed mental health professionals.

Precontemplation

INTERVENTION 1

Shoelaces

Assuming that awareness of a problem leads to automatic change is a common mistake. Awareness and acceptance of a problem are essential to creating change. But just being aware does not, by itself, create change. The most important ingredient to change is making changes. It's that simple, yet that challenging.

This activity is suitable for groups and individual clients.

Stages of Change: Precontemplation, contemplation, preparation, relapse.

Goal: Examine the impact of substance abuse and explore client's readiness for change.

Method: Client will gain insight as to how her substance use has impacted her relationships and will work to repair and strengthen healthy relationships.

What you will need: Shoes with shoelaces. You should wear them in case your client doesn't.

1. Begin with empathy. Welcome your client and ask about making changes. Ask questions like these:

    - *What does it mean to make a change?*

    - *How do you know you are ready to make a change?*

    If you are using this intervention in a group setting, ask each participant to briefly answer these questions, going around in a circle.

2. Introduce today's task: Getting ready to make changes. You can explain the process by saying:

    Have you ever postponed a task, perhaps homework or a big project at work, even though you knew the task was important and you would get in some sort of trouble if you did not complete it? It's really easy not to get started.

3. Review last week's homework: If you assigned a worksheet, ask to see it. If your client did not bring her worksheet, take out an empty worksheet and reflect together. If you are using this intervention in a group setting, go around the room and ensure that everyone gets an opportunity to reflect on last week's assignment. Always ask specific but open-ended questions. This will help your client find her own answers to questions about sobriety. Telling your client what is good for her can be tempting, but this implies that you do not trust her to find her own path to sobriety. Highlight any successes. If your client completed just a part of the assignment, that is still a success. If she was reluctant to complete the assignment but is able to talk about it, this is also progress, especially if your client has struggled with understanding reluctance in the past.

4. Work on today's task: Ask someone in session who is wearing shoes with laces to untie them. Then ask this person to walk around the room carefully (or do this yourself). Be very clear about the need to walk carefully. If the person is still walking recklessly, choose another person.

5. Say to the person: *"Your shoes are untied. I don't want to see you trip. However, don't tie your shoes, just keep walking."*

6. Listen for your client's response to this instruction. Is she laughing? Are you looking at confused faces in the group? Ask the person with untied laces to sit down.

7. Ask your client/group to reflect on what happened by asking questions like:

   - *What did you see?*
   - *Why did my instructions not make sense to you?*
   - *What do you think could happen here?*
   - *Why do you think you were laughing about the situation (if you were)?*
   - *What does this situation remind you of?*

8. Next, introduce the idea that making changes in recovery can relate to walking around with untied shoelaces. Ask:

   - *In what way is knowing that something is wrong helpful?*
   - *In what way is ongoing substance abuse like walking around with untied shoelaces?*
   - *How can you get from knowing about a problem (like substance abuse) to making changes?*
   - *What do you need to actually begin your recovery?*
   - *Who do you need by your side?*
   - *Who can't be there, because they will encourage you to "keep walking with untied shoes"?*
   - *What does it take to finally make the necessary changes (beginning recovery)?*
   - *In what way can people get stuck in the process of beginning their recovery?*

   In a group setting, you may want to divide the participants into subgroups by counting off numbers. Ask them to explore two of the questions and report back after about 10 minutes.

9. Listen and highlight the differences between thinking about changes and actually making changes and taking steps toward recovery. You can explain it like this:

   Thinking about recovery is important. It important to understand that substance abuse is a problem and to identify the problems it is causing in your life. At some point, though, it's time to "tie your shoes" to make the changes needed to begin recovery. Or you will keep on tripping!

   It's also important to mention that relapse is part of recovery. Having relapsed does not indicate one did not have enough insight about substance abuse or was not strong enough. Relapse is simply part of the illness.

10. Summarize: You have compared making changes in order to begin recovery with tying your shoes when you were walking around with untied shoes.

When your shoes are untied, it's easy to trip and you can't really run. If you do run, it's even easier to trip. You have explored what it would actually take to make changes.

Assign homework. Give your client the following index card to complete:

How I can take active steps to "tie my shoes" / commit to sobriety:

1.

2.

3.

The one thing I tried from the list above last week is:

Here is what happened when I tried:

Figure 3

11. Closing: Send your client/group home with words of encouragement like these: *You have already taken a great many steps toward recovery just by being here. Now it's time to try some new and active steps by giving sobriety a try. You can't know what it's like to be sober until you are sober.*

INTERVENTION 2

I Need...

Addiction makes users believe that it must be fed. Addiction constantly bombards us with messages telling us that we must obtain and consume the substance we crave. This intervention is designed to help your client begin to question the messages addiction sends.

This activity is suitable for groups and individual clients.

Stages of Change: Contemplation, action, maintenance, relapse.

Goal: Increase awareness of addiction to increase motivation for recovery-oriented change.

Method: Client will develop skills to manage thoughts, feelings, and situations without substance use.

What you will need: Paper, writing tools, markers, index cards, poster board image (see below).

1. Begin with empathy. Welcome your client and ask about the presence of things and people in his life that are not related to addiction. Ask questions like these:

   - *What did you do in the last week that had nothing to do with addiction?*

   - *Where did you go over the past few weeks that had nothing to do with addiction?*

   - *What kinds of conversations did you have over the last week that had nothing to do with your addiction?*

   Highlight any actions, activities, and conversations that were not related to your client's struggles with addiction and explain that there is, indeed, life after addiction that begins by taking small steps.

2. Introduce today's task: Beginning to question the messages about needing to use substances that addiction sends us. You can explain it like this: *Addiction tells us all kinds of things. They feel so true. But just because something feels true does not mean that it is true.*

3. Review last week's homework: If you assigned a worksheet, ask to see it. Read the worksheet together, or start with a new one. In a group setting, go around the room and ensure that everyone gets an opportunity to reflect on last week's assignment. Always ask specific but open-ended questions. This will help your client find his own answers to questions about sobriety. Telling your client what is good for him can be tempting, but this implies that you do not trust him to find his own path to sobriety. Highlight any successes. If your client completed just a part of the assignment, that is still a success. If he was reluctant to complete the assignment but is able to talk about it, this is also progress, especially if your client has struggled with understanding reluctance in the past.

4. Work on today's task: Remind your client or the group that addiction is a disease creating dependence on a substance and that this dependence affects our thinking and feeling.

5. Ask open-ended questions to explore beliefs about needing the substance in order to manage certain aspects of life:

   - *In your relationship with your partner, what do you think you could not do or manage without the substance?*
   - *In your relationship with your family, what do you think you could not do or manage without the substance?*
   - *At work or school, what do you think you could not do or manage without the substance?*
   - *With regards to your depression, anxiety, or trauma, what do you think you could not do or manage without the substance?*

6. Mount this image on a poster board to help your client/group understand that addiction is affecting all parts of life:

Figure 4

7. Provide paper and writing tools. Ask your client/group to copy the following sentence and complete at least one sentence related to each of the areas outlined in the graphic.

   I need________________ (name the substance)
   to________________ (name the action).

Provide the following examples to help your client/group members understand:

> I need *some oxy* to *get out of bed and make it through the workday.*

> I need *some alcohol* to *feel comfortable in the company of others because my anxiety is overwhelming without it.*

Give your client/group members 5–10 minutes to complete the sentences.

8. Ask your client/group to share their responses. In a group setting, explain that the group is a safe space where everyone gets to talk, one at a time. To ensure this, you should ask participants to go around the circle with their responses. Also explain that no feedback about the statements is needed right now.

9. Ask your client/group to stand up and jump just a little while saying repeatedly, "I cannot jump, I cannot jump, I cannot jump." Demonstrate how to do this, then engage in the activity together.

10. Ask your client/group to sit down and explore the activity together. You can ask:

    - *How is it that we can say something that is obviously not true?*
    - *Can you give an example of something you thought that was obviously not true?*
    - *Can you give an example of a feeling you had that did not fit the situation because it was based on something that was not really true?*

    Give the following example to illustrate:

    > *Jerry thought that his wife hated him because she did not greet him when he got home. He became really upset and began feeling awful. He started drinking to get rid of the awful feeling. Later he realized that his wife had fallen asleep.*

11. Now ask your client about the messages addiction sends. Ask:

    > *Which messages that addiction has sent you are not entirely true?*

    > *What are some ways you can respond to those messages when they are not entirely true?*

    > *How have you tried to ignore the messages addiction sends you in the past?*

    > *What has worked? What has not worked?*

12. Summarize: Your client/group members have considered that not everything we think or feel is necessarily true, and they have explored addiction's misleading messages.

13. Assign homework: Ask your client/group members to take an index card, write one of the sentences they created about needing the substance on the front of the card, and take it home. At the end of every day your client/group members should pick up the card and write one response to the statement on the back disproving the message addiction is sending. It's OK to

enlist family and friends. They should then bring the index card to the next meeting.

14. Closing: Send your client home with words of encouragement like these: *It's possible for you to talk back to addiction. It takes some practice. Over time it will become easier to dismiss the lies addiction is telling you.*

INTERVENTION 3

Problem or Solution?

Although it appears it would be easy to distinguish problems from solutions, it is not always clear. The cycle of addiction is the perfect example. Alcohol and drug use typically begin as a reward or as a solution to a problem. People typically use to feel good (adding a positive) or feel better (removing a negative). Over time, however, instead of it adding positive things and removing negative, it does the opposite. And due to the effects that addiction has on thought processes, the person does not see this clearly. A person with logical thinking would be able to identify that using alcohol and drugs has had an overall negative effect on their lives. The person with addiction does not believe this. Distortions are created to protect the addiction and to rationalize continued use. The supposed solution becomes the problem, but distorted thinking patterns make clients believe the only viable solution is to use more.

This activity is suitable for groups and individual clients.

Stages of Change: Precontemplation, contemplation.

Goal: Examine impact of substance use and explore client's readiness for change.

Method: Client will use motivational interviewing to explore substance use.

What you will need: Paper, writing tools, markers, index cards.

1. Begin with empathy. Welcome your client/group members. Ask:

   What is it like to be here?

   What are your feelings about being here?

   What part of you wants to be here?

   What part of you does not want to be here?

   Highlight any willingness to take new steps even if it is just the step to come to therapy today. Be careful not to be preachy about recovery. Your clients are probably hesitant about recovery. Try to connect to what they are bringing to the table.

2. Introduce today's task: Looking at what substance use has added to life and what it has taken away. Avoid words indicating judgment.

3. Review last week's homework: If you assigned a worksheet, ask to see it. Read the worksheet together, or start with a new one. In a group setting, go around the room and ensure that everyone gets an opportunity to reflect on last week's assignment. Always ask specific but open-ended questions. This will help your client find her own answers to questions about sobriety. Telling your client what is good for her can be tempting, but this implies that you do not trust her to find her own path to sobriety. Highlight any successes. If your client completed just a part of the assignment, that is still a success. If she was reluctant to complete the assignment but is able to talk about it, this is also progress, especially if your client has struggled with understanding reluctance in the past.

4. Work on today's task: Ask your client/group members to think back to the beginning of substance use, before it caused problems. Ask:

   - *What positive things did substance use add to your life?*
   - *What became easier?*
   - *What felt better?*

   Be sure to explain that it is necessary to go back to the beginning of substance use, before substance use caused any problems in life. Use a poster board to create a list of positives substances seemed to add to life. You may think that substance use never adds anything good to anyone's life, but this is simply not true. Maybe your client:

   - felt more at ease in social situations.
   - felt more courageous and was able to arrange for a date.
   - forgot about worries.

   Even though these things are short-lived, they initially added something to your client's life.

5. Ask your client to identify the first problem or set of problems or difficulties she experienced due to substance use. List these on the poster board. If your client struggles with this, ask what other people in her life would say. In this way your client does not yet have to own the problem but is beginning to talk about it. Don't try to convince her that the other people in her life are right. This will only alienate her and can lead to treatment refusal.

6. Ask when problems or difficulties began.

7. Pick one problem or difficulty and ask your client/group to take a step back from it. Ask them to imagine that a good friend of theirs had this problem. Ask them what they would say to this person. Here is an example: Perhaps your client has received his first citation for operating a vehicle under the influence. What would your client say to his best friend? What if it was the second citation? Role-play this with your client by acting as the best friend so that the client can give advice. In a group setting, pair up group members to role-play.

8. Process the role-play with your client/group. Ask:

   - *Did you take the step you asked your best friend to take?*
   - *If you did not, why didn't you?*
   - *What was addiction telling you to do?*

   Highlight the ways in which your client/group talk about using substances in order to address a problem or difficulty that substance use has created. Here is an example of what you can say: *It looks like you went out and got drunk after your first OVI because the OVI was just too much to think about. In what way has the problem (drinking) also become the solution (more drinking)?*

9. On another poster board, draw this image:

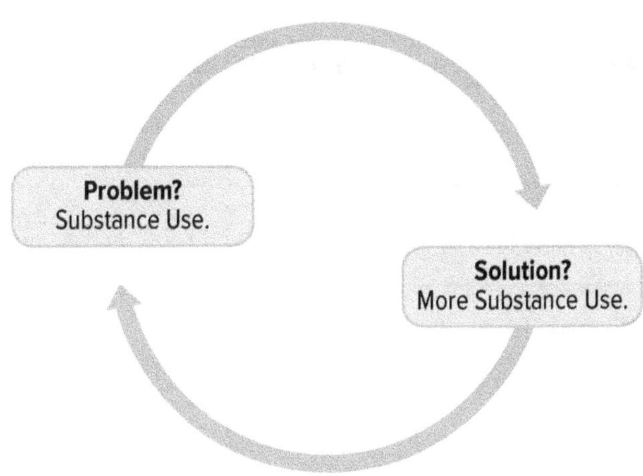

Figure 5

Ask your client/group how well this process works. Reflect back responses in a nonjudgmental way by saying things like this:

- *So what you are saying is that*_____________________________ (insert client response).

- *Is what you are telling me that* _____________________________ (insert client example of what is not working) *has caused some problems/difficulties?*

10. Use open-ended questions to elicit more information about the cycle of addiction in which the problem becomes an attempt at a solution. Find out which problem is causing your client so much trouble that she may be willing to consider recovery.

11. Summarize: You have explored how substance use can seem like the solution to the problems it creates.

12. Assign homework. Give your client/group the following worksheet to complete and bring back to your next meeting.

Things I have tried to limit my substance use or quit that did not work:
1
2
3
4
5
6
7
8
Underline any solutions that involved more substance use or led to more substance use.

Figure 6

13. Closing: Leave your client/group with words of encouragement like these: *It's human to want to get rid of difficulties. It's also possible to face difficulties. You can differentiate between a real and a temporary solution. Addiction tells you to choose addiction. You don't have to.*

INTERVENTION 4

Money, Money, Money...

Money can be a tricky subject for our clients even when they are not struggling with addiction. Most of our clients are marginalized and economically disadvantaged. There is never enough money to begin with. When addiction enters their lives, money takes on the all-important role of creating access to substances. When there is no money, addiction still demands to be satisfied. Many of our clients may have done things they never would have before addiction, and some of those things may involve illegal and traumatic activities such as stealing, dealing, and prostitution. Because money plays such as critical role in addiction, money itself can become a trigger for use.

This activity is suitable for groups and individual clients.

Stages of Change: Precontemplation, contemplation, preparation.

Goal: Increase awareness of addiction to increase motivation for recovery-oriented change.

Method: Client will use motivational interviewing to explore substance use.

What you will need: Paper, writing tools, markers, index cards, poster board. Images of $10, $50, and $100 bills glued on a poster board. Inexpensive piggy banks to give out.

1. Begin with empathy. Welcome your client/group members. Ask:

   - *Who crossed your path who made you feel respected or cared for?*

   - *Who crossed your path and you respected or cared for that person?*

   - *In what way are you holding on to what is important to you in spite of addiction?*

Highlight any compassionate or kind interactions. It is important that your client understands that even in the midst of addiction she is still worthy of respect and compassion.

2. Introduce today's task: Exploring and understanding the role of money in addiction. You can explain by saying:

   - *Addiction is very loud. It demands to be fed. Substance use calls for more substance use.*

   - *Drugs are cheap, at first. Then they become expensive.*

   - *It becomes harder to feed the habit.*

   - *Often, people spend a lot of time and effort to make money so that they can use.*

   - *Life becomes about money to feed the habit.*

3. Review last week's homework: If you assigned a worksheet, ask to see it. Read the worksheet together, or start with a new one. In a group setting, go around the room and ensure that everyone gets an opportunity to reflect on last week's assignment. Always ask specific but open-ended questions. This will help your client find her own answers to questions about sobriety.

Telling your client what is good for her can be tempting, but this implies that you do not trust her to find her own path to sobriety. Highlight any successes. If your client completed just a part of the assignment, that is still a success. If she was reluctant to complete the assignment but is able to talk about it, this is also progress, especially if your client has struggled with understanding reluctance in the past.

4. Work on today's task: Show your client the following image on a poster board:

Figure 7

Ask your client/group:

- *What are you thinking of when you look at the $10 bill?*
- *What about the $50 bill?*
- *What happens when you look at the $100 bill?*
- *What role did money play in your addiction?*
- *What role does it play now?*
- *In what way is money just money to you?*
- *In what way has it become a trigger for using substances?*

If your client develops strong cravings due to the sight of money, address this together by having her anchor herself in the here and now by looking at things and people in the room. Offer a soothing sensory experience such as a cup of warm tea or hot chocolate. Don't expect cravings to vanish quickly. Explain that this can take time.

5. Your client may describe illegal and traumatic experiences and activities when answering your questions. If you are using this intervention in a group setting, remind everyone that what is said in group stays in group.

6. If your client glamorizes past illegal activity, challenge this using Socratic questions like these:

    - *In what way did selling substances make your life more difficult?*

    - *In what way did you suffer because of prostitution?*

    - *How did your children's lives change because of your incarceration due to selling substances?*

    Be careful not to shame your client. Let her articulate the hidden costs of addiction.

7. Help your client/group explore the changing role of money in recovery. Ask:

    - *In what way can money itself remain a trigger?*

    - *How does your way of spending money change?*

    - *How do you spend your money now?*

    - *What are you no longer willing to do for money?*

    - *What can you do when money triggers you and you are at risk of using substances?*

    - *In what way is every day of sobriety money in the bank?*

8. Summarize: You have explored the ways in which money is central in addiction. Money becomes a way of obtaining substances; everything else comes later. You have discussed preparing for recovery by thinking of money as a means to gain access to basic needs and remembering that money can remain a trigger.

9. Assign homework. Give your client an inexpensive piggy bank. Ask her to write a short note each night about that day's relationship to sobriety and put this note in the piggy bank. Explain that thinking about sobriety and recovery is a way to put money in the bank. Ask her to bring the piggy bank to the next meeting.

10. Closing: Send your client home with words of encouragement like these: *Your relationship with money can change. It has already changed because you are not thinking about it only as a way to obtain substances. Every sober day and every day you walk toward sobriety is money in the bank of your life. Every sober day makes you richer!*

INTERVENTION 5

Prison Walls

This intervention is designed to help your client explore the ways in which addiction can become a prison. This activity is suitable for groups and individual clients.

Stages of Change: Contemplation, preparation, action, maintenance, relapse.

Goal: Increase awareness of addiction to increase motivation for recovery-oriented change.

Method: Client will gain insight as to how substance use has impacted relationships and will work to repair and strengthen them.

What you will need: Lots of cardboard boxes that can be stacked, enough to build a wall around your client. Paper, writing tools.

1. Welcome your client/group. Begin with empathy by saying things like this: *You made it here today in spite of addiction. Great job. Looks like you were able to ignore the messages addiction was sending you, at least temporarily. I am sure that was not easy. But you did it.*

2. Introduce today's task: Exploring the many ways in which addiction can become a prison even when we don't intend for this to happen. You can explain the task like this: *No one decides that they want addiction to isolate them. But addiction will build one wall at a time until we are trapped.*

3. Review last week's homework. If you assigned a worksheet, ask to see it. Read the worksheet together, or start with a new one. In a group setting, go around the room and ensure that everyone gets an opportunity to reflect on last week's assignment. Always ask specific but open-ended questions. This will help your client find his own answers to questions about sobriety. Telling your client what is good for him can be tempting, but this implies that you do not trust him to find his own path to sobriety. Highlight any successes. If your client completed just a part of the assignment, that is still a success. If he was reluctant to complete the assignment but is able to talk about it, this is also progress, especially if your client has struggled with understanding reluctance in the past.

4. Work on today's task: Ask your client to build three walls out of cardboard boxes. Ask your client to step into the structure, then ask for permission to build a final wall that will enclose him. The walls should be too high to see over, and the interior space should be just big enough to accommodate the person. (This intervention is not suitable for someone who struggles with claustrophobia.) In a group setting, the group can work together to build the structure, and you can ask for a volunteer to step inside.

5. Ask the person inside:

    - *What does it feel like to be inside the structure?*

    - *How long do you think you will feel comfortable in this structure?*

    - *What can't you do because you are inside the structure?*

In a group, invite everyone to ask their own questions. Then gently knock down the walls.

6. Help your client/group reflect on the ways in which addiction has imprisoned them by asking:

    - *What have you not been able to do because of the prison of addiction?*
    - *Who have you not been able to see because of the prison of addiction?*
    - *In what ways have you begun to break out of the prison of addiction?*
    - *What part of you is still behind the walls?*
    - *What would it take to help that part of you break out?*

7. Summarize: You have explored the ways in which addiction can become a prison.

8. Assign homework: Give your client the following index card to complete and ask him to bring the card back to your next meeting:

Steps I can take to leave the prison of addiction:

1. _______________________________________

2. ____

3. ____

Figure 8

9. Leave your client/group members with words of encouragement like these:

    - *Keep in mind that the outside world is always there, even when you feel cut off from it.*
    - *Building connection with those who are not imprisoned by addiction can help you find a way out of the prison of addiction.*
    - *There are people who want to help you get out of the prison of addiction.*

Contemplation

INTERVENTION 6

My Foundation 💜

When building a sense of mastery in recovery, it is important to help your client begin to develop self-awareness. You can help your client with this by helping her explore what makes her unique.

This activity is suitable for groups and individual clients.

Stages of Change: Precontemplation to preparation.

Goal: Develop client-driven recovery plan.

Method: Client will utilize motivational interviewing to explore substance use.

What you will need: White board and white board marker or large piece of paper and markers.

1. Begin with empathy. Welcome your client. Ask about the prior week. Make it clear that you are happy your client is here with you and/or has returned to treatment. You can say things like this:

   - *I am so happy you are here.*

   - *I respect that you came today.*

   - *I understand that just coming here took effort.*

   Listen reflectively and validate client feelings and thoughts. Keep in mind that validation is not the same as agreement!

2. Introduce today's task: Exploring and understanding your client's foundation, her sense of self, including what is important to her. You can use the term "values" if your client can relate to it.

3. Work on today's task: Draw a line down the middle of the paper or whiteboard and ask your client to begin thinking about what is needed to build a house. You can ask Socratic questions like these:

   - *Where do you begin when you build a house?*

   - *What happens when you begin to build in the wrong area?*

   - *Why don't we begin building a house by putting up some drywall?*

   - *What would you say if someone started to build their house without pouring a foundation?*

   If you are using this intervention with a group, be sure to make sure that everyone listens and lets everyone else finish. Remind participants that everyone will get their turn, and it is important to let others finish.

   As you are exploring how your client would build a house, highlight your client's attempts to ensure that the house is built on a solid foundation. You can say things like this:

   - *It's a great idea to make sure that your house has a solid foundation.*

   - *This will keep the house stable.*

   - *This house will be built well and won't be easily blown over.*

Ask your client to begin drawing the house, step by step, in the order in which a house would be built. When your client has completed the house drawing, help her reflect on it. If you are using this intervention with a group, the entire group can reflect on how to build a solid house.

4. Now ask:

    - *What do you need to build a solid foundation for your life?*

    - *What do you already have in place?*

    - *What has worked in the past?*

    - *What have you neglected that is important to you?*

    - *What foundation supports your sobriety and recovery?*

    Give your client an opportunity to elaborate. Highlight your client's areas of strengths, particularly when she does not believe she has any strengths and has not done anything right in the past. You can say things like this:

    - *You have talked a lot about how important your children are to you. Love and connection are a great foundation.*

    - *You just talked about how hard you work. Hard work can be a great foundation for recovery because recovery is hard.*

5. Summarize: You have explored the idea of building a house on a solid foundation. You have begun to identify your client's foundation for her life and recovery.

    Added spiritual component of intervention step.

    Ask your client:

    - *In what way do you feel connected to a higher power or purpose?*

    - *Who or what has carried you through your darkest times?*

    - *How can your higher power be your foundation and support you?*

6. Assign homework. Send your client home with the following worksheet:

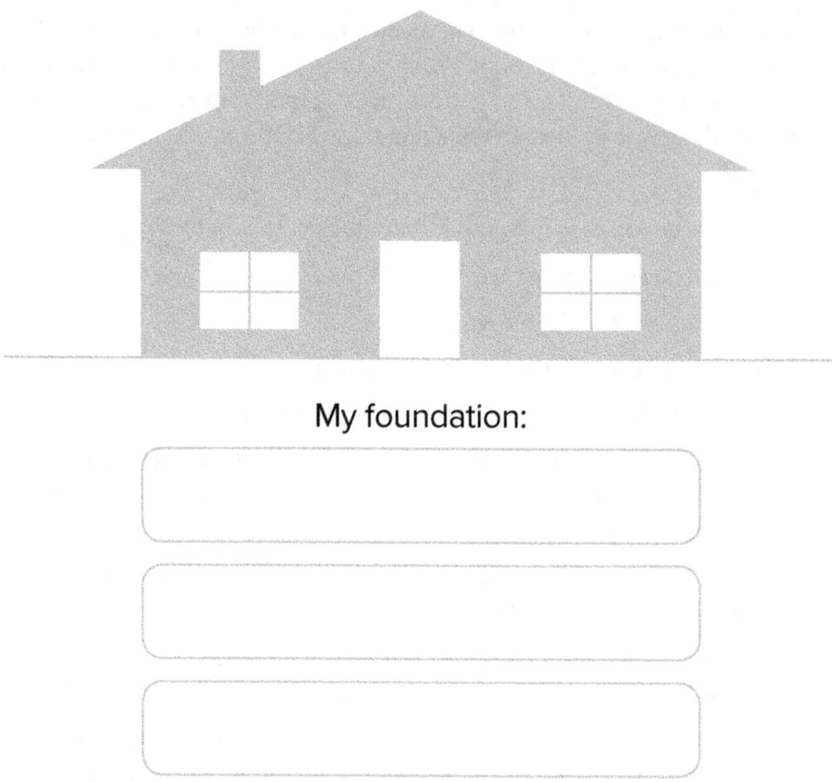

My foundation:

Figure 9

7. Closing: Ask your client to bring the completed worksheet to your next meeting. Send her home with words of support like these: *You already have a foundation. You can build on this foundation. You can build a better life.*

    In a group, you can ask each member to close with a brief word of support for everyone. Make sure that you are the last person to speak to ensure that the group closes with definite words of encouragement.

INTERVENTION 7

The Tower of Recovery

Thinking about sobriety and long-term recovery can be daunting. The following intervention can help your client, in a playful way, be more flexible in thinking about recovery.

This activity is suitable for groups and individual clients.

Stages of Change: Preparation, action, maintenance.

Goal: Develop client-driven recovery plan.

Method: Client will increase communication, decision-making, and problem-solving skills.

What you will need: Old newspapers and magazines, lots of tape, scissors.

1. Begin with empathy. Welcome your client and ask who was supportive of his recovery in the past week. Ask questions like:

   - *Who noticed that you were working hard to stay sober?*

   - *What did it feel like that someone was paying attention to your hard work?*

   - *Who did you have to step away from because they were not supportive?*

   Highlight your client's successes and ability to reflect on sobriety and recovery. Be mindful: Success does not always mean that sobriety is achieved—for many it means beginning to think about sobriety.

2. Introduce today's task: Becoming creative and flexible about building sobriety. Provide psychoeducation by saying things like:

   - *Sobriety often requires us to develop new skills.*

   - *Addiction may tell us to do the same thing over and over.*

   - *Making change is difficult. Becoming more flexible can be tough.*

   - *We often need help when we build sobriety. Accepting help can be tricky because addiction may have told us to keep secrets.*

3. Review last week's homework: If you assigned a worksheet, ask to see it. In a group setting, go around the room and ensure that everyone gets an opportunity to reflect on last week's assignment.

4. Work on today's task: In a group setting, separate participants into groups of three to four. Each group will receive paper, tape, and a pair of scissors to construct a free-standing structure that reaches the ceiling. The structure cannot be taped to the floor or ceiling. Ask the groups to simply wait quietly for the other groups to finish once they are finished.

5. Give an opportunity to ask questions about the task and answer them.

6. While all groups are working, have a notepad ready. Listen to challenges the groups experience. Here are some things to pay attention to:

   - Does each group have a leader who takes control?

   - Do all team members participate? Cooperate?

- Do the groups interact?

- Is there competition among groups?

- Are teams making changes to the structure as it grows? Do they need to go back and reinforce it?

- Do groups learn from each other?

- What does it seem to take to be effective in completing the task?

7. Once everyone has completed the task, or when a reasonable amount of time has passed, begin processing the activity. Ask:

    - *What did you need to complete this activity? How did you need to be with each other?*

    Read back quotes you jotted down during the activity referring to doubts that it could be completed or the need to work together. Help the group reflect on what the activity is about? Ask:

    - *How does this activity relate to recovery?*

    - *Why do we need to work together in recovery?*

    - *What happens when people do not work together to support each other's recovery?*

    - *Is everyone working toward a common goal?*

    - *How important is it to be flexible and open to trying new things in recovery?*

    - *What can happen when we become competitive about recovery?*

    Don't provide answers. You want your client/group to express in their own words how recovery can work for them. Telling answers is much less effective than experiencing them!

8. Summarize: You have learned about principles of recovery by building the Tower of Recovery. You have learned that flexibility and cooperation is needed, that building together is much better than building alone, that it is good to learn from each other and ask for help, and that it feels good to support each other.

9. Assign homework: Give your client the following worksheet to complete at home with the help of a friend, family member, or sponsor.

The Tower of Recovery

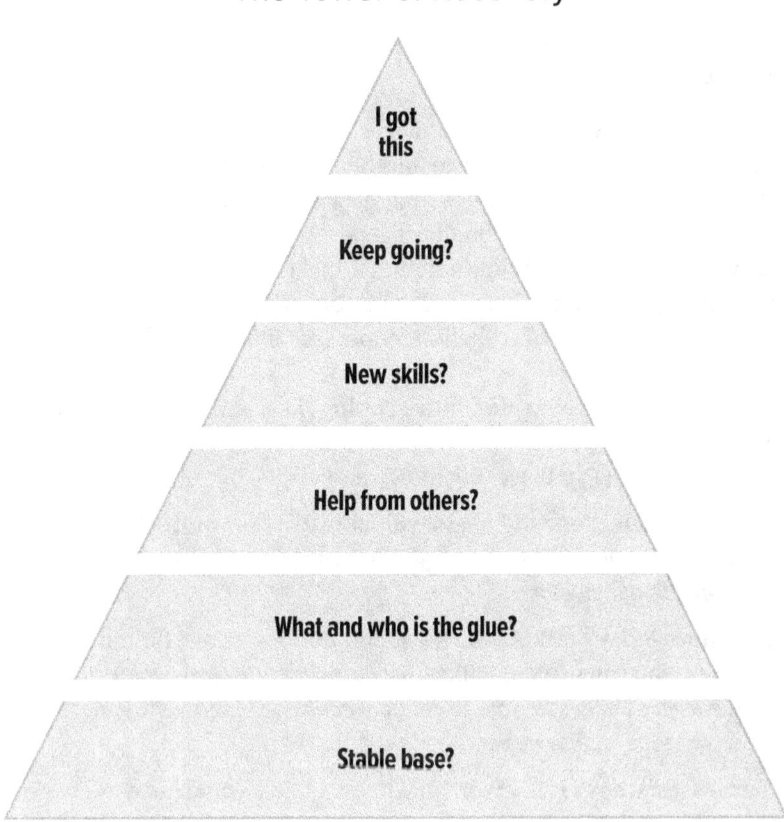

Figure 10

Ask your client to name at least one action, behavior, situation, or person that supports his Tower of Recovery for each section of the tower and bring the worksheet back to your next meeting.

10. Closing: In a group setting, ask everyone to say something encouraging to the person to their left. If you need to, you can give examples like these:

    - *You don't have to do this alone.*

    - *We are building a stable base for recovery together.*

    - *Sometimes we all have to rebuild. That's OK.*

    - *It's important to keep going, step by step.*

INTERVENTION 8

The Bridge

This intervention uses the metaphor of a bridge. Bridges connect things. We have to cross bridges to get from one place to another. Sometimes bridges cross small streams, and sometimes they cross canyons. Moving from active addiction to recovery can mean crossing over a canyon of triggers.

This activity is suitable for groups and individual clients.

Stages of Change: Contemplation, preparation, action, maintenance.

Goal: Increase awareness of addiction to increase motivation for recovery-oriented change.

Method: Client will develop alternative coping skills and implement them to manage stressors and triggers.

What you will need: Paper, writing tools, markers.

1. Welcome your client and begin with empathy. Say things like this: *It can be tough to get on the road to recovery. There can be many obstacles. But we are here to figure this out together.*

2. Introduce today's task: Using the metaphor of a bridge for the recovery journey. You can explain it like this: *Recovery can take us through difficult territory. We have bridges to cross to get from addiction to recovery. Bridges are useful. They make the journey easier.*

3. Review last week's homework. If you assigned a worksheet, ask to see it. Read the worksheet together, or start with a new one. In a group setting, go around the room and ensure that everyone gets an opportunity to reflect on last week's assignment. Always ask specific but open-ended questions. This will help your client find her own answers to questions about sobriety. Telling your client what is good for her can be tempting, but this implies that you do not trust her to find her own path to sobriety. Highlight any successes. If your client completed just a part of the assignment, that is still a success. If she was reluctant to complete the assignment but is able to talk about it, this is also progress, especially if your client has struggled with understanding reluctance in the past.

4. Work on today's task: Give your client/group a large piece of paper and markers. Ask them to draw a bridge from their imagination. Explain that it does not have to be perfect. If anyone struggles with perfectionism, provide reassurance that the drawing will not be judged for beauty or accuracy. This should only take about five minutes or so.

5. Ask how the bridge could be a metaphor for the journey of recovery. Here are some questions you can ask:

    - *What are you leaving behind?*

    - *Who are you leaving behind?*

    - *Which way are you going?*

- *What is on the other side?*

- *What are you hoping will be on the other side, if you can't see it yet?*

Ask your client/group to write the answers on the bridge. Help your client/group be as specific as possible about this by prompting her to think about:

- people

- places

- things

- feelings

- relationship patterns

- abilities

- difficulties

6. Explore where your client is in relation to the bridge of recovery. Looking at it? About to step on it? Crossing it? Approaching the other side? Mark the spot with the date.

7. Expand on the metaphor of the bridge by reminding your client/group that bridges have railings for a reason. Ask them to identify their supports that keep them from falling off the bridge. Ask them to write the names of the supports on the paper.

8. Ask about and discuss obstacles on or around the bridge and have her draw them by the bridge. Process what your client/group members bring up. There could be a rock to trip over. There could even be a sign by that road pointing in the wrong direction.

9. Ask your client about her strengths and have her write those strengths on the paper.

10. Summarize: You have explored the metaphor of the bridge to guide your exploration of the recovery journey. You have identified roadblocks and barriers, but also strengths and supports.

11. Assign homework: Ask your client to cross a small bridge that leads toward recovery every day. Send home five index cards with the image of a small bridge. You can use this image:

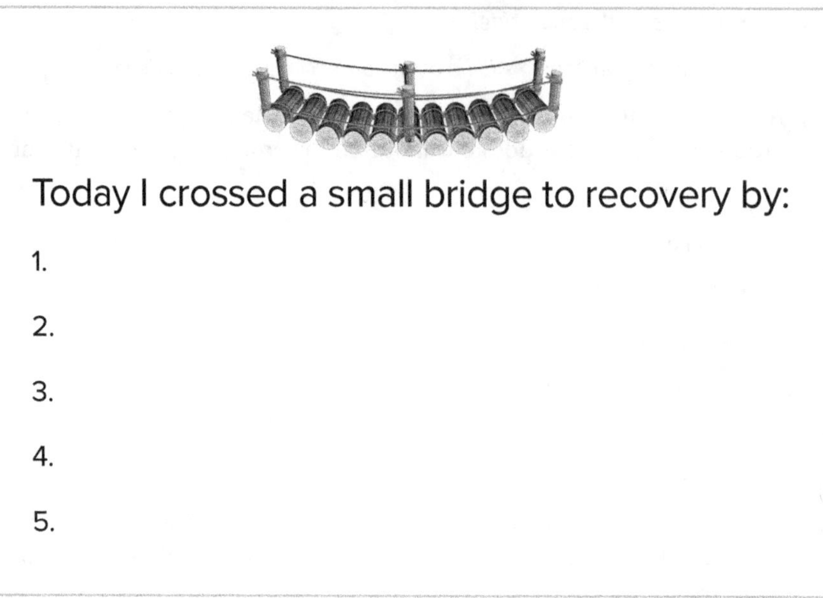

Figure 11

       Ask everyone to bring the index cards back to your next meeting.

12. Closing: Send your client home with words of encouragement like these: *Every step toward or on the bridge counts. Obstacles are part of the journey. You can keep walking in spite of obstacles. There is support to cross the bridge.*

INTERVENTION 9

Best Friend and Worst Enemy

In many ways, addiction feels great, at least in the beginning. The dulling of pain, both physical and emotional, can create a feeling of freedom from what has formerly weighed us down. In that way, addiction feels like a best friend. But addiction demands more and more of us—time, money, values, priorities. Addiction becomes our worst enemy, and we lose the freedom we thought addiction gave us. This intervention is designed to help your client feel the tension between the promise and realities of addiction.

This activity is suitable for groups and individual clients.

Stages of Change: Contemplation, preparation, action, maintenance.

Goal: Increase awareness of addiction to increase motivation for recovery-oriented change.

Method: Client will use motivational interviewing to explore substance use.

What you will need: Paper, writing tools, markers, poster board.

1. Begin with empathy. Welcome your client and tell him that you are happy to see him. In a group setting, welcome the group as a whole by emphasizing connections between members: *I am so happy to see how all of you are supporting each other. Coming here is a commitment to your recovery and to everyone's recovery. The support for each other will benefit all of you.*

2. Identify today's task: Exploring how addiction can turn on you, from seemingly being your best friend to becoming your worst enemy. Explain that no one would pick up a substance if it did not seem to make some things better, at least temporarily.

3. Review last week's homework: If you assigned a worksheet, ask to see it. Read the worksheet together, or start with a new one. In a group setting, go around the room and ensure that everyone gets an opportunity to reflect on last week's assignment. Always ask specific but open-ended questions. This will help your client find his own answers to questions about sobriety. Telling your client what is good for him can be tempting, but this implies that you do not trust him to find his own path to sobriety. Highlight any successes. If your client completed just a part of the assignment, that is still a success. If he was reluctant to complete the assignment but is able to talk about it, this is also progress, especially if your client has struggled with understanding reluctance in the past.

4. Work on today's task: Ask your client/group to explore their closest friendship from the time before they began struggling with addiction. You can ask:

   - *When did you first meet this friend?*

   - *How did you feel when you met this friend?*

   - *How did you know that you were going to be friends?*

   - *What did you do together that created a bond between the two of you?*

- *How did your friend help you when you were struggling?*

- *How did you help your friend when he was struggling?*

While your client/group members are exploring the answers to these questions one by one, take notes on a poster board or worksheet like this:

How my best friend has supported and helped me:
1.
2.
3.
4.
5.
6.
7.
8. and so forth.

Figure 12

5. Ask your client to name all the words on the list that are related to help, connection, values, positive experiences. Say them out loud as you highlight them by putting them in the following sentence:

    So what you are saying is that a best friend will/will not _______________ (insert best friend's action).

6. Create a list of promises addiction has made on a poster board, then help your client/group examine which promises were kept, for how long, and when they were broken.

7. Role-play the situation of addiction offering friendship. You can personify addiction and your client/group members can be themselves. When you are in the role of addiction, promise a lot. Say things like this:

    - *I can make you feel soooo much better.*

- *You will never have to feel sad or mad again.*

- *Everything will be all right. I will take care of everything.*

- *No more sadness and fear.*

- *Forget about your family and friends. They just weigh you down.*

- *I will make you so much better!*

Watch how your client/group members respond. Then promise even more things, such as success in relationships. You may want to begin to slur your speech a bit as you make these promises. Keep watching responses.

8. Ask your client/group what part of addiction's promises sounded, and maybe still sound, tempting, and when they began to have doubts. Ask:

    How does this happen? How does addiction turn from seemingly taking care of everything to putting you on the path to losing everything? When did you feel the first pull in the wrong direction? How difficult is it to recognize the first pull in the wrong direction?

9. Help your client/group explore ambivalent feelings about addiction. Don't try to bury them. Listen and validate.

10. Ask your client/group to think again about their best friend. Ask: *Would you recommend addiction to your best friend? Why or why not?*

11. Then ask if that best friend (who may or may not still be in this person's life) would recommend addiction to them. You may want to go back to the list of helpful things best friends do. Say:

    None of you talked about your best friend making you ill. I don't see anything about your best friend asking you to lose your job or house or children. Friendships are healing relationships. They make us better.

12. Summarize: You have explored ways in which addiction presents itself as a friend who takes care of everything, then betrays that friendship.

13. Assign homework. Ask your client to use the following worksheet to find a way to end the friendship with addiction by telling it about the ways in which it has betrayed him. He should bring the worksheet back to your next meeting.

<table>
<tr><td>Ways in which addiction has betrayed my friendship:

</td></tr>
<tr><td>Addiction has asked me to:

</td></tr>
<tr><td>Addiction has led to:

</td></tr>
<tr><td>Since addiction became my friend I:

</td></tr>
<tr><td>Here is what I would like to say to addiction to alter our relationship:

</td></tr>
</table>

Figure 13

14. Closing. Send your client/group home with words of encouragement like these: ***True friendships are healing relationships. You are deserving of true friendships.***

INTERVENTION 10

The Ladder of Recovery

This intervention uses the metaphor of climbing a ladder out of the pit of addiction. When you are struggling with addiction, it's hard to put much effort into anything other than obtaining and consuming substances. It's difficult to climb the ladder, especially when some of the rungs are loose and you repeatedly fall back down. But in the long run it's worth the effort.

This activity is suitable for groups and individual clients.

Stages of Change: Relapse.

Goal: Obtain skills to maintain sobriety.

Method: Client will increase knowledge of relapse process, identification of triggers to relapse, and relapse-prevention skills.

What you will need: Image of a ladder with rickety steps.

1. Welcome your client and begin with empathy by saying: *Recovery is both amazing and hard work. You are here doing the work of recovery. We are here to support each other in the work of recovery because the work can be so hard.*

2. Introduce today's task: Exploring why it is important to keep climbing the ladder of recovery, even after slipping back down a step or two. You can explain it like this: *When you are working on your recovery it can feel like gravity is always pulling you back down toward addiction. If you fall, you may be so hurt that you can't even locate the ladder. But that does not mean the ladder is not there.*

3. Review last week's homework: If you assigned a worksheet, ask to see it. Read the worksheet together, or start with a new one. In a group setting, go around the room and ensure that everyone gets an opportunity to reflect on last week's assignment. Always ask specific but open-ended questions. This will help your client find her own answers to questions about sobriety. Telling your client what is good for her can be tempting, but this implies that you do not trust her to find her own path to sobriety. Highlight any successes. If your client completed just a part of the assignment, that is still a success. If she was reluctant to complete the assignment but is able to talk about it, this is also progress, especially if your client has struggled with understanding reluctance in the past.

4. Work on today's task: Show your client/group the following image:

Figure 14

Ask:

- *In what way is addiction like being down in a pit?*
- *How far away does anything that is not in the pit of addiction seem?*
- *What is it like to start climbing the ladder of recovery?*
- *When have you slipped back down a step or two?*
- *How did it feel to slip back down?*
- *What motivated you to keep climbing?*
- *In what way did addiction try to keep you from climbing?*
- *Who can help you fix the ladder?*
- *What can you do if you need more than a ladder to climb out of the pit of addiction?*

Highlight any responses that illustrate the need and willingness to keep climbing and to ask for help with a broken ladder. You can say: *When you are struggling with addiction, fixing a ladder is tough because thinking well is tough. Sometimes you need to ask for help with fixing the ladder.*

5. Ask your client/group who or what makes the climb worth it. What is waiting up above? Highlight all responses that help your client look forward to a stable and meaningful life with healthy relationships. You can say things like this:

- *You are looking forward to having* _______________________________ (insert name of trusted friend/partner/children) *back in your life.*
- *You are looking forward to not having to chase the next high.*

- *You are looking forward to people trusting you again.*

- *You might be looking forward to just having a life, going to work, not being afraid all the time.*

6. Emphasize that when you are climbing the ladder of recovery, you are both climbing away from something and climbing toward something.

7. Summarize: You have explored how difficult climbing out of the pit of addiction can be, especially when you fall back down a few steps because of a relapse. You have explored what motivates you to keep climbing.

8. Assign homework: Ask your client/group to create a drawing or collage of all the things they are moving toward when climbing up the ladder of recovery and to bring it to your next meeting. Explain that the drawing is not about drawing a perfect picture, but rather creating an image that will motivate continued movement toward recovery. You can explain that it is also OK to create a collage.

9. Send your client/group home with words of encouragement like these:

    You have come so far. You may have already slid back down the ladder a couple of times, but here you are, still climbing. When you are climbing or getting back on the ladder you are moving toward recovery one step at a time. Every step counts.

Preparation

INTERVENTION 11

What Matters

The following intervention is designed to help your clients explore and understand what matters to them in order to help them identify their values. But the term "values" can be off-putting, so it's best to refer instead to "what matters." Later you can introduce the term *values* to see if it fits in your clients' contexts. Values identification can help your client find intrinsic motivation for change.

This activity is suitable for groups and individual clients.

Stages of Change: Precontemplation, contemplation, preparation.

Goal: Develop client-driven recovery plan.

Method: Client will increase communication, decision-making, and problem-solving skills.

What you will need: Index cards, pen, paper, small trash can.

1. Begin with empathy. Welcome your client and ask who responded positively to changes he made over the past week. Ask questions like these:

   - *Who supported you when you discussed becoming sober?*

   - *How did you respond to this support?*

   - *How did you communicate with others, even just a little bit, about your decision to become sober?*

2. Introduce today's task: Identifying what matters most to your client. Explain that what matters most can drive recovery. You can explain by saying:

   > *We all have things that matter to us. These are things like family, children, our achievements, our friends. We try to put the things that matter to us first. When we do that, using substances is no longer in first place!*

3. Review last week's homework: If you assigned a worksheet, ask to see it. Read the worksheet together, or start with a new one. In a group setting, go around the room and ensure that everyone gets an opportunity to reflect on last week's assignment. Always ask specific but open-ended questions. This will help your client find his own answers to questions about sobriety. Telling your client what is good for him can be tempting, but this implies that you do not trust him to find his own path to sobriety. Highlight any successes. If your client completed just a part of the assignment, that is still a success. If he was reluctant to complete the assignment but is able to talk about it, this is also progress, especially if your client has struggled with understanding reluctance in the past.

4. Work on today's task: Begin by explaining:

   > *The things that matter to us tend to make us do things, like get out of bed in the morning to make breakfast for the kids when we really don't want to get up yet. It's important to figure out what matters to us. They can help us in our recovery because they can make us do things that are tough to do, such as turn away from an offer to use substances. Some things that matter are*

also embedded in our culture, such as freedom, trust, honesty, and stability. These are things that matter to a lot of people.

5. Give your client ten index cards. If you are using this intervention in a group setting, give each client 10 index cards. Instruct your client to write one value on each. Some clients may have difficulty with identifying ten values. This is OK. In a group setting, participants can help each other. You can also help with questions like:

   - *What made you get out of bed this morning?*
   - *The last time you had to do something you did not want to do, what made you do it?*
   - *What do you believe in? What is really important to you?*
   - *Who is really important to you and why? It's OK if you have not had contact with that person for a while. They can still be important to you.*

6. Once your client has ten cards completed, pick up the small trash can and ask him to throw three cards he is willing to part with into the basket—these would be things that are important to him, but not high on the list of importance.

7. Ask what it was like to let go of some things that are important to him. In a group setting, remind everyone that the group is a judgment-free zone and only one person should talk at a time. Go around the circle to give each participant an opportunity to talk.

8. Then ask your client to throw another three cards into the trash can and to reflect on his choices. Again, ask your client to reflect on what it was like to let go of some of the things that matter to him. Keep going until he has only one card left. Ask why he kept that one.

9. Help your client explore how addiction can take away our focus on what matters to us. Ask: *Have you ever lost a job, money, a relationship, or your freedom because of addiction?*

10. Make sure that your client does not start shaming himself for letting go of things that matter to him and that group participants do not shame each other. You can say: *Addiction often lies and tells us that the things that truly matter to us do not matter. Addiction tells us this loudly and in our face. Believing addiction is not a personal weakness—it's just part of the process of addiction.*

11. Ask if anyone has kept sobriety or recovery as the last card. Ask the following questions:

    - *Why do you have to prioritize sobriety and recovery in order to hang on to the other things that matter to you?*
    - *What happens if you don't?*

Remember, don't tell your client the answers. Trust his innate ability to figure this out for himself.

12. If your client asks if he can have some of the cards he threw into the trash back, ask why and what he would be willing to try to get them back.

13. Summarize: Your client has identified what matters to him and has let those things go, one by one of what matters. He has reflected on what addiction can take away. He has explored the importance of putting recovery and sobriety first so he can hold on to what matters the most to him.

14. Assign homework: Ask your client to identify one thing that he can do to prioritize sobriety over the next week and to write it on an index card. Ask him to look at this card every morning and evening and to give himself a checkmark if he engaged in the sobriety-prioritizing activity that day.

Figure 15

Ask your client to bring the card to your next meeting.

15. Closing: Send your client home with words of encouragement like these: *You already know what matters to you. This is a great foundation. Now you just have to make those things a priority. You made a great plan to start with this.*

INTERVENTION 12

Superhero

This intervention is designed to help your client identify and use her inherent strengths to become her own superhero—not necessarily by doing extraordinary things all the time, but rather by recognizing her willingness and capacity to take steps to save herself from addiction.

This is a two-part intervention. The next intervention will help your client explore and accept the need to have all kinds to superheroes in her life to assist her with her recovery.

This activity is suitable for groups and individual clients.

Stages of Change: Contemplation, preparation, action, relapse.

Goal: Develop a client-driven recovery plan.

Method: Client will develop alternative coping skills and implement them to manage stressors and triggers to substance use.

What you will need: Any superhero costume or cape. Images of common super-heroes. Poster board and marker.

1. Begin with empathy. Welcome your client and ask about making changes. Ask questions like these:

    - *In what way did having an addiction trip you up last week?*

    - *What went well because you made changes?*

    If you are using this intervention in a group setting, ask each participant to briefly answer these questions, going around in a circle.

2. Introduce today's task: Recognizing and activating the superhero within. You can explain the task like this:

    > *We have within us the ability to be our own superheroes. Addiction may lead us to believe that we can't ever quit and that there is nothing we can do to save ourselves. But this is really not true. Being your own superhero just means taking steps toward sobriety and recovery every day. You may not be able to fly, but you can be your own hero.*

3. Review last week's homework: If you assigned a worksheet, ask to see it. Read the worksheet together, or start with a new one. In a group setting, go around the room and ensure that everyone gets an opportunity to reflect on last week's assignment. Always ask specific but open-ended questions. This will help your client find her own answers to questions about sobriety. Telling your client what is good for her can be tempting, but this implies that you do not trust her to find her own path to sobriety. Highlight any successes. If your client completed just a part of the assignment, that is still a success. If she was reluctant to complete the assignment but is able to talk about it, this is also progress, especially if your client has struggled with understanding reluctance in the past.

4. Work on today's task: Help your client explore her idea of a superhero by asking questions like these:

- *Who is your favorite superhero?*

- *What does your favorite superhero do that you admire?*

- *What qualities does your favorite superhero have that you admire?*

In a group setting, give each participant a chance to answer each question. You may want to hang up or pass around a list or images of popular superheroes just in case there is someone who is not familiar.

5. Ask your client to identify a quality in herself that relates to one of the qualities of her favorite superhero, even if just a little bit. Write that quality on the poster board in big, bold letters. If you are using this intervention in a group setting, go around the circle and give each person an opportunity to answer. Use your poster board to create a list of qualities.

6. Then ask your client to identify something she does that relates to one of the helpful things the superhero does even if just a little thing. Write this item in big bold letters on the poster board. If you are using this intervention in a group setting, go around the circle and give each person an opportunity to answer. Use your poster board to create a list of superhero-like actions.

7. Help your client explore ways in which she can use her superhero-like qualities and actions to help her own recovery. As questions like these:

    - *How can you use your ability to be_________________* (insert superhero-like quality) *to aid your own recovery?*

    - *How can you use your ability to _________________* (insert superhero-like action) *to aid your own recovery?*

8. If your client objects to being called a superhero, help her understand that being a superhero really just means being helpful to others, not being a bystander when things are dire.

9. Ask your client to put on the superhero cape. In a group setting, each participant should get a chance to put on the cape, and they should clap for each other. Ask group members to clap for each other when they are putting on the cape. If you are working with an individual client, provide positive feedback for the ways in which your client is already her own hero.

10. Summarize: You have helped your client explore and understand which superhero-like qualities she already has and what superhero-like actions she already takes. You have then bestowed upon your client the superhero cape.

11. Assign homework: Give your client the following index card.

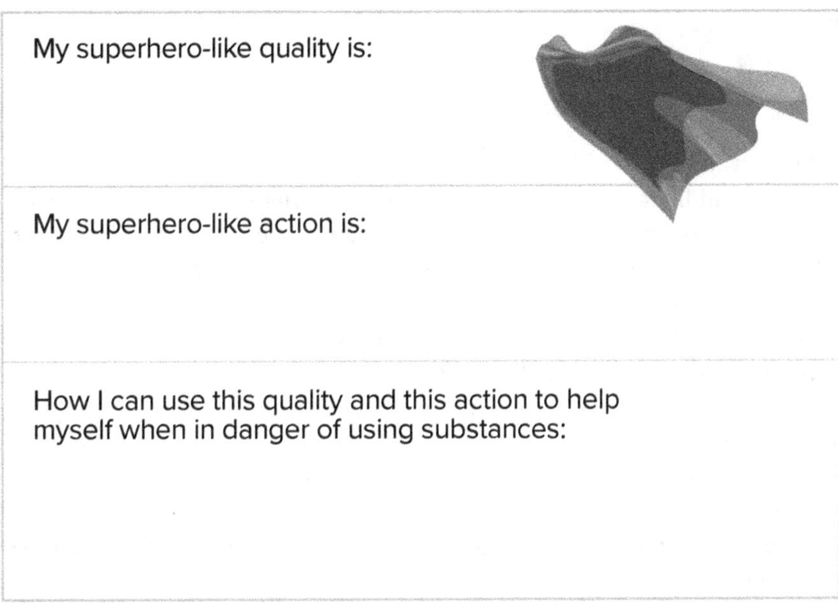

Figure 16

Ask your client to fill in the blanks, then carry the card every day and review it when she is struggling with the urge to use. Ask her to bring the card back to your next meeting.

12. Closing: Send your client/group home with words of encouragement like: *You already have the ability to help yourself. You can be your own superhero. You can take small steps to help yourself.*

INTERVENTION 13

The Planet of Addiction

Living with addiction could be described as living on a different planet. Someone living in active addiction does not have the same experiences as someone who doesn't. It can be helpful for someone contemplating recovery to identify the differences between the two worlds. Recognizing that addiction truly sends you to another planet can be a catalyst for change.

This activity is suitable for groups and individual clients.

Stages of Change: Contemplation, action, maintenance, relapse.

Goal: Increase awareness of addiction to increase motivation for recovery-oriented change.

Method: Client will develop skills to manage thoughts, feelings, and situations without substance use.

What you will need: Paper, writing tools, markers, index cards, poster board with planet image.

1. Begin with empathy. Ask your client/group about moments of peace they had over the past week, no matter how brief. Ask them to describe this moment in detail. If you see his face relaxing or a faint smile on his face, point this out after your client has finished talking by saying: *I notice that when you talk about* _________________ (describe peaceful moment) *your face* _____________ (describe impact of moment on facial expression).

2. Introduce today's task: Recognizing the many ways in which addiction has sent you to another planet in which the rules and ways of living are very different.

3. Review last week's homework. If you assigned a worksheet, ask to see it. Read the worksheet together, or start with a new one. In a group setting, go around the room and ensure that everyone gets an opportunity to reflect on last week's assignment. Always ask specific but open-ended questions. This will help your client find his own answers to questions about sobriety. Telling your client what is good for him can be tempting, but this implies that you do not trust him to find his own path to sobriety. Highlight any successes. If your client completed just a part of the assignment, that is still a success. If he was reluctant to complete the assignment but is able to talk about it, this is also progress, especially if your client has struggled with understanding reluctance in the past.

4. Work on today's task: Take out a poster board that looks like this:

Figure 17

5. Ask the following questions:

  - *What do you do on the planet of addiction that you would not do on another planet?*

  - *What does a typical day look like on the planet of addiction?*

  - *In what ways does the planet of addiction itself look different?*

  - *What is the terrain like?*

  - *What is missing on the planet of addiction?*

  - *Who else lives on the planet of addiction?*

As your client/group give answers, write them on the planet.

6. When all answers are recorded, ask:

  - *How do you feel when you look at this planet?*

  - *If you had a spaceship and fuel, would you leave?*

  - *What would it take to leave this planet?*

7. Summarize: Your client has described what the planet of addiction looks like and what it's like to live there. He has also explored how people act on this planet and what the environment is like.

8. Assign homework: Give your client/group a worksheet containing the following image:

Figure 18

Ask your client/group to write or draw on the image what happens on this planet and bring the worksheet to your next meeting.

9. Closing: Send your client/group home with words of encouragement like these:

> *You can think about getting off the planet of addiction. You can take steps to get off the planet of addiction. When you work together on getting off the planet of addiction you have already taken a great step.*

INTERVENTION 14

Walls Up!

In our lives, healthy boundaries are needed. We can't always be there for everyone, we like to have our own spaces, and we tend to share intimate information only with those we are close to. Addiction isolates. It changes what we share. Addiction tells us to replace fences with walls—not to protect us, but to protect the addiction. This intervention is designed to help your client explore and understand ways in which she has put up walls between herself and others in order to protect her addiction.

This activity is suitable for groups and individual clients.

Stages of Change: Contemplation, preparation, action, maintenance, relapse.

Goal: Increase awareness of addiction to increase motivation for recovery-oriented change.

Method: Client will gain insight as to how her substance use has impacted her relationships and will work to repair and strengthen healthy relationships.

What you will need: Large blocks or cardboard boxes that can be stacked, enough to build a wall. Paper, writing tools.

1. Welcome your client and begin with empathy by using words like:

   Living with addiction can be hard because addiction eats up all your time and money. It can't be easy to be you right now. But you are in good company. People recover; they reconnect. You are well on your way just by being here.

2. Introduce today's task: Exploring and understanding how addiction creates barriers between us and people we were formerly connected to. You can explain:

   You probably had friends or family you were close to before addiction took over. Addiction has a way of taking those people from us. When we are struggling with addiction, we often have to hide parts of our lives that are related to it. As addiction grows, we hide more and more of our lives. This is isolating. And it's hard to recover when living an isolated life.

3. Review last week's homework: If you assigned a worksheet, ask to see it. Read the worksheet together, or start with a new one. In a group setting, go around the room and ensure that everyone gets an opportunity to reflect on last week's assignment. Always ask specific but open-ended questions. This will help your client find her own answers to questions about sobriety. Telling your client what is good for her can be tempting, but this implies that you do not trust her to find her own path to sobriety. Highlight any successes. If your client completed just a part of the assignment, that is still a success. If she was reluctant to complete the assignment but is able to talk about it, this is also progress, especially if your client has struggled with understanding reluctance in the past.

4. Work on today's task: Give your client/group the large blocks or cardboard boxes. Ask them to build a wall in the middle of the room.

5. Ask your client to sit behind the wall so that you can't see her. Then ask her to use facial expressions to show you how she is feeling. In a group setting, ask for a volunteer to sit behind the wall. The rest of the group will sit on the other side of the wall with you.

6. Explore why it is hard to know how the person behind the wall is feeling. Ask:

   - *How do we know how someone is feeling?*

   - *How do we feel when we can't figure out how someone is feeling?*

   - *What do you think can happen to the person behind the wall if we can't connect with her?*

7. Next, ask your client or another group member to go behind the wall and engage in an activity without talking about it. Then explore why it is hard to know what the person behind the wall is doing. Ask:

   - *How do we know what someone is doing?*

   - *How do we feel when we can't figure out what someone we care about is doing?*

   - *What do you think can happen to the person behind the wall if we can't connect with her?*

8. Knock down the structure together so the person behind the wall can be seen again.

9. Help everyone explore how the wall can be a metaphor for living with addiction by asking:

   - *What walls have you put up since you started living with addiction?*

   - *When did you build higher walls?*

   - *Who was able to climb over the wall and help you in spite of the wall?*

   - *When you are behind the wall of addiction, when are you looking for help with tearing down the wall?*

10. Summarize: You have explored the many ways in which addiction builds walls between us and family and friends. You have begun to think about how these walls may need to be broken down in order to recover from addiction.

11. Assign homework: Give your client the following index card and ask her to bring it back to your next meeting.

Ways in which I can begin to tear down the wall:

1. ______________________________

2. ______________________________

3. ______________________________

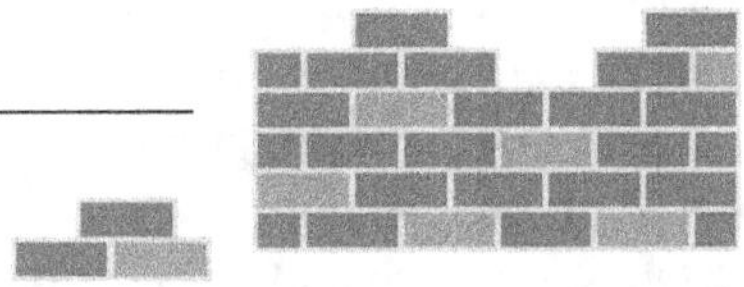

Figure 19

12. Closing: Send your client home with words of encouragement like these: ***If you can build walls you can tear them down. You may need a hammer. You may ask for help from the people on the other side of the wall.***

INTERVENTION 15

Don't Talk, Don't Trust, Don't Feel...

Addiction has a way of taking over all aspects of life, including relationships. Addiction tells us to isolate ourselves from others in order to maintain itself. Surely those around us who care about us would want to help us recover from addiction if they knew fully about our struggles. Things become even more complicated when several family members struggle with addiction or when it has become a family disease, perhaps over several generations. In this case the messages addiction sends us, such as "don't talk, don't trust, don't feel," are deeply embedded into family patterns, including how children are taught to manage their feelings, thoughts, and relationships. But not feeling, not trusting, and not talking further raise the risk of developing or maintaining addiction.

This activity is suitable for groups and individual clients.

Stages of Change: Action.

Goal: Obtain skills to maintain sobriety.

Method: Client will increase communication, decision-making, and problem-solving skills.

What you will need: Paper and markers.

1. Welcome your client and begin with empathy. Say things like this:

   It's hard when addiction tries to dictate every aspect of your life. You have to work hard every day to ignore the messages that addiction sends you. That can be tiring. But we are here to support you. Together we are stronger.

2. Introduce today's task: Questioning addiction's messages and creating new and more positive messages about our life with others, messages that sustain recovery. You can explain it like this:

   Addiction tells us all kinds of things that are not necessarily true but seem true. Addiction tells us not to trust others, and this isolates us. We become used to isolation. But isolation protects addiction. It does not protect us.

3. Review last week's homework: If you assigned a worksheet, ask to see it. Read the worksheet together, or start with a new one. In a group setting, go around the room and ensure that everyone gets an opportunity to reflect on last week's assignment. Always ask specific but open-ended questions. This will help your client find his own answers to questions about sobriety. Telling your client what is good for him can be tempting, but this implies that you do not trust him to find his own path to sobriety. Highlight any successes. If your client completed just a part of the assignment, that is still a success. If he was reluctant to complete the assignment but is able to talk about it, this is also progress, especially if your client has struggled with understanding reluctance in the past.

4. Work on today's task: Show your client/group the following image:

Figure 20

Ask:

- *What do you see?*
- *What do you think this image is about?*
- *When have you felt that you needed to be silent?*
- *When have you tried to avoid seeing something?*
- *When have you felt like you needed to cover your ears because you did not want to hear something?*
- *How does not talking, seeing, hearing, trusting, and feeling connect with addiction?*

Listen and amplify any responses that make a connection between severing human connections and addiction. Rephrase those responses to emphasize how isolating addiction really can be. You can say things like this:

- *So what you are saying is that it's easier to be quiet and blend in so no one asks about your drinking.*
- *Is what you mean that it's best to shut off your feelings when you are using; otherwise you would feel really guilty?*

5. Next, help your client/group explore the upside of not talking, seeing, hearing, trusting, and feeling. Ask:

   - *What do you get out of not feeling, communicating, etc.?*
   - *How does shutting down work for you?*

6. Then, help your client/group explore the cost of not talking, seeing, hearing, trusting, and feeling. Ask:

   - *What happens when you shut this part of you down?*
   - *What do you miss about yourself when you are in this shut-down mode?*
   - *What do you miss about others?*
   - *What happens to your relationships when you are in shut-down mode?*
   - *What happens to your willingness to be on the road to recovery?*

Don't try to tell your client/group about the negative impacts of shutting down. Let them describe it themselves.

7. Ask your client to pick a relational skill or ability and reflect on what would happen in a specific situation if he could use this skill. You can use the questions below. In a group setting, pair up members and as them to interview each other using the following questions:

- *What is the specific situation in which you have shut down a skill or ability that connects you with others because of addiction?*

- *What would have happened if you had not shut that skill down?*

- *What opportunities for connection would have come up?*

- *How would these opportunities have helped you move toward recovery?*

- *In what way would you have made changes to the situation if you had not been in shut-down mode?*

Highlight any responses that explore how increased communication and trust can lead to better connections with others. If your client brings up painful emotions that emerge when reconnecting with others, explain that feelings, too, can be accepted and managed with the help of others.

8. Summarize: You have explored how addiction shuts down important ways of connecting with others, such as communication, trust, and feelings. You have explored the upside of this but also the enormous cost of not feeling and connecting.

9. Assign homework: Give your client the following index card to take home, complete, and then bring to your next meeting:

<table>
<tr><td>

This week I will: ____
(insert one of the following: see, hear, speak, trust, feel)

when I am with: ____
(insert person)

</td></tr>
<tr><td>

Here is how it went:

</td></tr>
</table>

Figure 21

10. Send your client home with words of encouragement like these: *It's possible to trust again, talk again, and feel again. It will take time and practice. And it's OK to make mistakes.*

Action

INTERVENTION 16

In the Mirror

This intervention can be used to help clients with seeing who they are, inside and out. It helps them see that they are more than their addiction, and that they still have positive qualities that can be identified, nurtured, and sustained through recovery.

This activity is suitable for individual clients and single-gender groups. (Men and women can have very different responses to their reflections.)

Stages of Change: Preparation, action, maintenance, relapse.

Goal: Increase awareness of addiction to increase motivation for recovery-oriented change.

Method: Client will develop skills to manage thoughts, feelings, and situations without substance use.

What you will need: Mirror.

1. Begin with empathy. Welcome your client and ask about changes related to giving up substances. Ask questions like these:

   - *When did you turn away from an opportunity to use substances?*

   - *How did it feel to do so?*

   - *What made it possible for you not to use? What did you do differently?*

   If your client explains that she relapsed, help her identify other opportunities she had to use but didn't. Help her recognize past successes, no matter how small.

2. Introduce today's task: Recognizing inner beauty and potential hidden by addiction.

3. Review last week's homework: If you assigned a worksheet, ask to see it. Read the worksheet together, or start with a new one. In a group setting, go around the room and ensure that everyone gets an opportunity to reflect on last week's assignment. Always ask specific but open-ended questions. This will help your client find her own answers to questions about sobriety. Telling your client what is good for her can be tempting, but this implies that you do not trust her to find her own path to sobriety. Highlight any successes. If your client completed just a part of the assignment, that is still a success. If she was reluctant to complete the assignment but is able to talk about it, this is also progress, especially if your client has struggled with understanding reluctance in the past.

4. Work on today's task: Begin by explaining that this intervention can bring up strong feelings. Remind your client that you are there for her. In a group setting, remind members of the importance of supporting each other and ask for a volunteer for this intervention. You can say things like: *You are not alone. We are all here to support each other in recovery. Each person's recovery journey is different. It's important to see the beauty of our recovery journeys.*

5. Ask your client if you can hold a mirror in front of her and ask questions about what she sees. When she gives her answers, affirm that you are seeing the same thing as long as her answers are just descriptive, not judgmental. In a group setting, ask other group members to affirm client responses.

6. Ask what she sees inside of herself. At this point many clients will begin to make judgmental statements about themselves. If this happens, provide positive feedback about what you see. In a group setting, ask members to give feedback, too. Remind everyone that group is a judgment-free zone.

7. As your client explores how she sees herself both externally, using the mirror, and internally, reflecting on what is unseen, help her identify positive qualities that were present before her addiction began by asking:

   - *What did you appreciate about yourself before you began using substances?*

   - *What did others appreciate about you before you began using substances?*

   - *Which of those qualities are still there inside of you?*

   - *When do you see those positive qualities, even if just briefly?*

   - *How can you nurture those positive qualities?*

   - *What can others do to nurture those qualities?*

8. When your client brings up negative things she sees in herself, remind her that no one is perfect, and relate them back to her addiction when appropriate. To illustrate your point, say something like this:

   Jill tends to lose her temper quickly when she is using substances. When she is sober, Jill can be patient with her children and her friends. Jill tends to refer to herself as mean, but her struggles with her temper are really related to her addiction.

9. Additionally, be sure to reiterate that no one is perfect—with or without an addiction. It's OK to have flaws.

10. Ask the following questions to help your client (or the group) reflect on her self-image:

    - *Which of the things you see in yourself are related to who you really are?*

    - *Which of the things you see in yourself right now are related to your addiction?*

11. Summarize: You have explored visible and invisible qualities together. You have identified negative qualities that have developed because of addiction. You have explored that it is OK not to be perfect.

12. Assign homework. Give your client or group members the following index card to take home, complete, and bring to your next meeting:

Positive qualities about myself that can't be seen at first glance:

1. ____

2. ____

3. ____

4. ____

5. ____

Figure 22

Your client should identify at least two positive qualities and then interview family or friends to identify more. Remind her that positive qualities can be little things such as being a good listener or being able to comfort a child.

13. Closing: Send your client home with words of encouragement like:

> *We all have beautiful qualities, even if they are hidden. They are still there. It's important to remind ourselves that we have these beautiful qualities. Sometimes others need to help us with this.*

INTERVENTION 17

The Letter

For clients in the active stage of working on recovery, taking stock can be helpful. Reviewing what they have already accomplished can help your clients recognize achievements they may otherwise downplay, and may help them develop a sense of self-efficacy that will be helpful for the future.

This activity is suitable for groups and individual clients who are past the preparation stage.

Stages of Change: Action, maintenance, relapse.

Goal: Maintain recovery-oriented behaviors.

Method: Client will develop skills to manage thoughts, feelings, and situations without substance use.

What you will need: Paper and writing tools, flat surface to write on.

1. Begin with empathy. Welcome your client and ask about changes related to giving up substances. Ask questions like these:

   - *What is it like to go through a series of days without using substances?*

   - *How are those days different?*

2. Introduce today's task: Writing a letter to someone close to and younger than the client, detailing struggles and successes in recovery. You can explain that this can be helpful to young people.

3. Review last week's homework: If you assigned a worksheet, ask to see it. Read the worksheet together, or start with a new one. In a group setting, go around the room and ensure that everyone gets an opportunity to reflect on last week's assignment. Always ask specific but open-ended questions. This will help your client find his own answers to questions about sobriety. Telling your client what is good for him can be tempting, but this implies that you do not trust him to find his own path to sobriety. Highlight any successes. If your client completed just a part of the assignment, that is still a success. If he was reluctant to complete the assignment but is able to talk about it, this is also progress, especially if your client has struggled with understanding reluctance in the past.

4. Work on today's task: Give your client or group members a pen, paper, and a flat surface to write on. In a group setting, ask everyone not to talk with each other.

5. Ask your client to tell his story of recovery, truthfully recounting his struggles and his steps toward sobriety. Explain that the letter should highlight that addiction can happen to anyone, that he has come far, and, most importantly, that he has made it through to recovery. The idea is to show younger family members and friends that recovery is possible. Encourage your client to include details, but not ones that could trigger cravings in himself or others. This is, of course, difficult to gauge. You also want to be sure that

everyone in this group is, at least at this moment in time, past the preparation stage of change.

6. Give your client or the group fifteen to twenty-five minutes to write this letter. Pay close attention to literacy. If your client can't write well or is not comfortable with writing, he can draw or create a cartoon. Explain that it is OK to take time to think about the letter. Also, that the letter does not have to be perfect. You can say:

   - *Just write as you would talk.*

   - *This is not a formal letter.*

   - *It's more like telling a story.*

   - *It's OK to draw to illustrate your story if that is more comfortable.*

   - *Try not to judge yourself while writing, as this is a judgment-free zone.*

7. When they're done writing, invite everyone to share their letters. Listen intently and don't interrupt. Then, highlight accomplishments by saying things like:

   - *It's amazing how far you have come.*

   - *I am so glad you made it through.*

   - *Your younger friends/family members are so lucky to have you to tell them about your recovery.*

   - *It's amazing that you can now support others.*

   Encourage the group to give positive feedback to each reader. Continue until everyone who is willing has shared. Suggest to those who aren't willing to read aloud in the group to share the letter with an individual counselor.

8. Ask if they thought, at the beginning of recovery, that they could come this far. Give them an opportunity to reflect on the answer.

9. Explain that communicating with the next generation about addiction and recovery is a great gift your client can give, but that he should not feel responsible for the recovery journey of another person. You can say:

   Every journey is different. You can send your wisdom out into the world, but you can't dictate their journey. The best message we can send into the world is to continue to maintain recovery. This is the strongest message we can send.

10. Summarize: Your client has written a letter to his younger friends and family members recounting his journey of addiction and recovery. By telling his story of addiction and recovery he has sent a message to the next generation about the possibility of recovery. He has also learned to recognize his tremendous achievements.

11. Assign homework: Send your client home with the letter he wrote. Ask him to read the letter to himself at least once, and to a close friend or family member at least once. Give your client the following index card to mark homework completion.

Read letter to myself:	Completed?	Read letter to a friend/family member:	Completed?
How did I feel when I read the letter to myself?			
What feedback did I get when I read the letter to a family member/friend?			

Figure 23

12. Closing: Send your client/group home with words of encouragement like: *Sharing your story of addiction and recovery was a courageous thing to do. Recognize how far you have come!*

INTERVENTION 18

Superheroes

This intervention builds on the prior superhero intervention. In order to reach and maintain recovery we do have to become our own superheroes, but we also need others to help us. Addiction, however, is inherently isolating. Addiction can convince us that we can or need to do everything, including recovery and sobriety, by ourselves. This belief can harm the recovery process.

This activity is suitable for groups and individual clients.

Stages of Change: Contemplation, preparation, action, relapse.

Goal: Develop a client-driven recovery plan.

Method: Client will develop alternative coping skills and implement them to manage stressors and triggers to substance use.

What you will need: Any superhero costume or cape. List of common superheroes with images. Poster board and marker.

1. Begin with empathy. Welcome your client and ask about making changes. Ask questions like these:

    - *In what way were you your own friend over the last week?*

    - *What did you say to yourself to soothe yourself when you were upset or tempted to use substances?*

    - *What worked?*

    In a group setting, ask each participant to briefly answer these questions, going around in a circle.

2. Introduce today's task: Recognizing our need to let other superheroes help us. You can explain it like this: *It may seem like we have to do this all by ourselves. But this is just not true. We all need help and support.*

3. Review last week's homework. If you assigned a worksheet, ask to see it. Read the worksheet together, or start with a new one. In a group setting, go around the room and ensure that everyone gets an opportunity to reflect on last week's assignment. Always ask specific but open-ended questions. This will help your client find her own answers to questions about sobriety. Telling your client what is good for her can be tempting, but this implies that you do not trust her to find her own path to sobriety. Highlight any successes. If your client completed just a part of the assignment, that is still a success. If she was reluctant to complete the assignment but is able to talk about it, this is also progress, especially if your client has struggled with understanding reluctance in the past.

4. Work on today's task: Tell your client the following story:

    There once was a man who was very good at everything. He was a great father, was well respected at work, was good looking, and people thought highly of him. But then something changed. The changes happened over a period of time so at first he did not notice. It was harder for him to get out of bed in the morning. He was often exhausted. He hardly ate and felt sick when he did. His wife and children began to feel like a burden.

Over a period of several months, things got harder and harder. He began missing work. Both his boss and his wife expressed concerns about his well-being and offered to help him, but he refused any offers for help. Being strong and independent was very important to him, and he was not going to let anything or anyone help him.

Finally, he reached a point at which he could no longer get out of bed.

Ask your client or group what they think may be going on with the man. Ask:

- *What do you think is happening?*
- *What are the clues that something is not right?*
- *What do you think about the man's decision not to accept any help?*
- *Who all is affected by the man's decision not to accept any help?*

Help your client or group consider several possibilities about what may be going on, not just one.

5. Continue to tell the story:

    Finally, an old friend who had not seen the man for a long time stopped by after hearing that he was not well. When the friend saw the man, he was in shock and said: "You, my friend, are very, very sick. I don't know what exactly is going on, but I am going to call an ambulance right now." The man did not object; he was too tired and sick. The friend took decisive action and, by doing so, saved the man's life. It turned out that the man had become severely anemic and needed help right away. Because of his old friend's help, he recovered. When he returned home after his hospital stay, he phoned his old friend and thanked him by saying, "You are my hero."

6. Ask your client or group what they think about the friend's actions. Ask:

- *What did the friend do right?*
- *Why do you think others close to the man did not take the same action?*
- *Why do you think the man did not object to the help this time?*
- *In what ways were the old friend's actions heroic? In what way were they just logical?*

In a group setting, form smaller groups and assign each one question. Let them discuss for about 10 minutes, then report back to the full group.

Highlight any reflection about the need to accept help from others, no matter how independent we would like to be. Help your client make the connection between the story and her situation by asking the following questions:

- *In what way is addiction like the man's illness?*
- *In what way is it not?*

- *What do you think would have happened to the man if the old friend had not stopped by?*
- *What do you think could happen to someone who is alone and too proud to accept help when struggling with addiction?*
- *What advice would you have given the man when he was beginning to get sick?*
- *What advice would you give someone who is beginning to struggle with substance abuse?*

Help your client or group reflect on these questions and highlight that humans just need each other, that we really can't do everything alone.

7. Summarize: You have shared the story of a man who became gravely ill and refused help from others until it was almost too late. You have compared the man's illness with the disease of addiction and have explored the need to accept help from others.

8. Assign homework: Give your client or group members the following worksheet to complete at home:

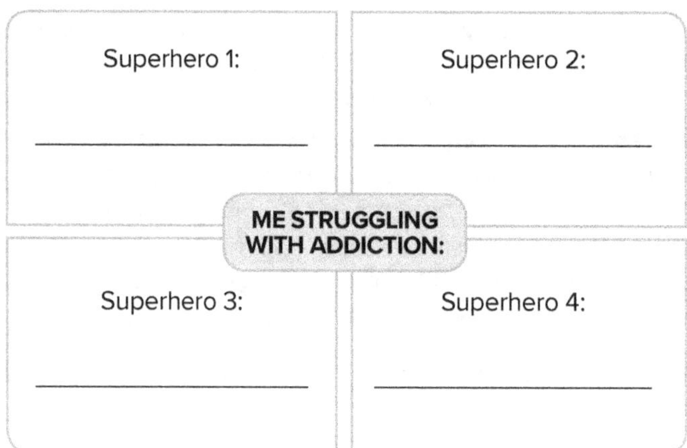

Figure 24

Ask your client to name at least three people who have come to her aid during her struggle with addiction. Then ask her to contact at least one of those people and tell them about the ways in which they have been helpful in recovery. Finally, tell your client to ask that person if she could call again when she is struggling with the urge to use substances.

9. Closing: Send your client/group home with words of encouragement like these: *You have the ability to ask for help. You can let others be your superhero. You can take small steps to let others help you.*

INTERVENTION 19

Standing Strong

To maintain sobriety, we need to develop and maintain important supports in our lives. Supports can be people, like sponsors, family, and friends. They can also be activities like working out or being part of a team, or they can be specific coping skills, such as sticking to a routine that supports sobriety.

This activity is suitable for groups and individual clients.

Stages of Change: Action, maintenance.

Goal: Maintain recovery-oriented behavior changes.

Method: Client will learn refusal skills, decrease association with other substance users, and increase associations with sober support.

What you will need: Paper, writing tools, markers, index cards, poster board.

1. Begin with empathy. Welcome your client/group members and ask:

    - *How did you begin, maintain, or move back toward sobriety in the past week?*

    - *What was tough?*

    - *What situation or experience, no matter how small, gave you hope?*

2. Introduce today's task: Building and maintaining a wide network of sup-ports. Explain that supports can come in the form of people, such as spon-sors and friends; activities, such as membership in a team; and habits designed to cope with intense feelings related to challenges to sobriety. Here are some examples of supports:

    - sponsor

    - best friend

    - pet

    - daily routine

    - bowling team

    - books

3. Review last week's homework: If you assigned a worksheet, ask to see it. Read the worksheet together, or start with a new one. In a group setting, go around the room and ensure that everyone gets an opportunity to reflect on last week's assignment. Always ask specific but open-ended questions. This will help your client find her own answers to questions about sobriety. Telling your client what is good for her can be tempting, but this implies that you do not trust her to find her own path to sobriety. Highlight any successes. If your client completed just a part of the assignment, that is still a success. If she was reluctant to complete the assignment but is able to talk about it, this is also progress, especially if your client has struggled with understanding reluctance in the past.

4. Work on today's task: Give your client the following image on a worksheet:

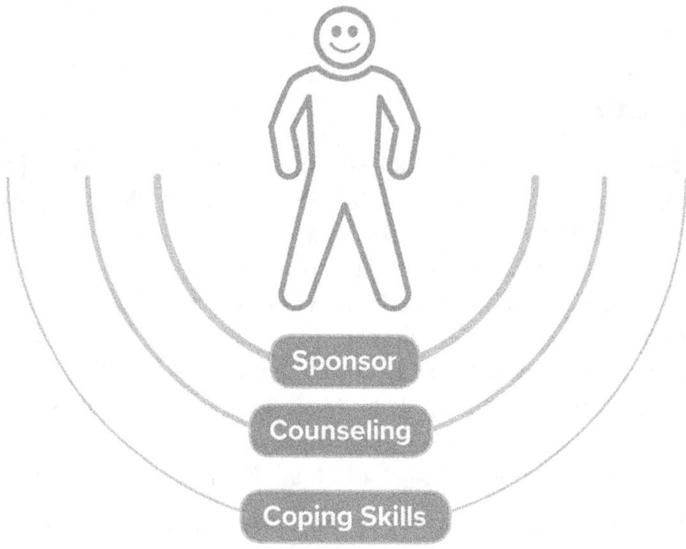

Figure 25

Explain that everyone needs a support network. You can also call it a safety net. Say: *Recovery is a long and hard journey. Part of the joy of the journey is that we don't have to travel alone. In fact, we really can't. It's too dangerous. We need someone or something to catch us when we fall.*

5. Ask your client to add to the image above by indicating everyone and everything that is part of her safety net. She can write or draw her network of support. Give your client/group some time to add as many supports as they need and have.

6. If your client feels that she is missing a support component, ask her to draw an empty box and indicate with a red marker what is missing.

7. Explore with your client what she has done with her safety net and provide positive feedback for building it. Explore any additional safety needs indicated in red and help your client close the gaps in the safety net. In a group setting, ask each member to explore at least one element of their safety net with the other group members.

8. Ask your client or group to indicate the person they can turn to when in danger of relapse.

9. Summarize: You have explored the need to have a support network of people, activities, pets, and things to help prevent relapse. Explain again that relapse is part of addiction and everyone needs to plan for it.

10. Assign homework. Give your client the following index card to complete and bring to your next meeting.

My Safety Net Needs More:

1. ____

2. ____

3. ____

Figure 26

Ask your client to pick one item off that list and integrate it into her safety net over the next week.

11. Closing: Send your client home with words of encouragement like these: *We all need someone or something to lean on. You are doing a great job being supportive to yourself. Now, let others support you and support others.*

INTERVENTION 20

Protection ♥

This intervention has an integrated spiritual component as it refers to something or someone greater than the individual struggling with addiction. Use this intervention with a client or group that is open to the idea of a higher power. This power does not need to fit neatly into traditional ideas of faith or religion.

This activity is suitable for groups and individual clients.

Stages of Change: Action, maintenance.

Goal: Develop client-driven recovery plan.

Method: Client will develop alternative coping skills and implement them to manage stressors and triggers.

What you will need: Paper, writing tools, markers, index cards, poster board.

1. Begin with empathy. Ask your client:

    - *When were you offered support in the last week?*

    - *Who offered support?*

    - *How did you feel about being offered support?*

    - *How difficult is it for you to accept support?*

2. Introduce today's task: Noticing and accepting support and protection from a power or idea greater than ourselves. You can explain:

    We are all connected with each other. To many this connection between us is sacred. We understand that together we are more than the sum of our parts. In the same way we may feel a connection with a power or idea greater than us. Some people refer to this idea as a higher power, and some name that power according to their religious or faith traditions. Either way, the idea of a higher power or purpose often incorporates the idea of protection. This idea can be helpful when we are struggling with addiction, which often puts us into dangerous situations.

3. Review last week's homework: If you assigned a worksheet, ask to see it. Read the worksheet together, or start with a new one. In a group setting, go around the room and ensure that everyone gets an opportunity to reflect on last week's assignment. Always ask specific but open-ended questions. This will help your client find his own answers to questions about sobriety. Telling your client what is good for him can be tempting, but this implies that you do not trust him to find his own path to sobriety. Highlight any successes. If your client completed just a part of the assignment, that is still a success. If he was reluctant to complete the assignment but is able to talk about it, this is also progress, especially if your client has struggled with understanding reluctance in the past.

4. Work on today's task: Ask your client/group to listen to the following story:

    There once was a child, a small child who was full of adventure. Every day he tried to escape the care of his mother, and every day she protected him in ways he was not aware of. When he ran toward the road close to their house she scooped him up playfully and carried him to the backyard. When he tried to open the front door at night, she began to lock it to make sure he did not end up outside in the cold and the dark. When he did not want to wear a hat out in the snow, she bought him ear warmers. She protected him every step of the way as much as she could.

5. Pause and ask your client/group the following questions:

   - *Who has protected you in the past?*

   - *Who has not protected you?*

   - *How do you feel when someone tries to protect you?*

   - *Who do you think has tried to protect you without you noticing?*

   - *In what way does the space of therapy provide protection for you?*

   - *In what ways do other people, maybe even the people present now, provide protection for you?*

   - *In what way have you felt protected by a power or idea larger than yourself?*

   Listen reflectively. Highlight any ideas your client voices about protection. In a group setting, give each member the opportunity to answer at least one of the questions. Emphasize that everyone's idea of a higher power or purpose is different and will be respected, and that it is also OK not to think about it.

6. Next ask:

   - *How has your higher power or purpose protected you when you were in the depth of addiction?*

   - *How can a connection with a higher power or purpose protect you now and help you in your recovery?*

   Encourage your client/group to connect their answers with vivid memories or hopes for the future.

7. Summarize: You have explored the idea that humans need protection and that a higher power or purpose can offer this sense of protection.

8. Assign homework: Give your client/group the following worksheet to complete:

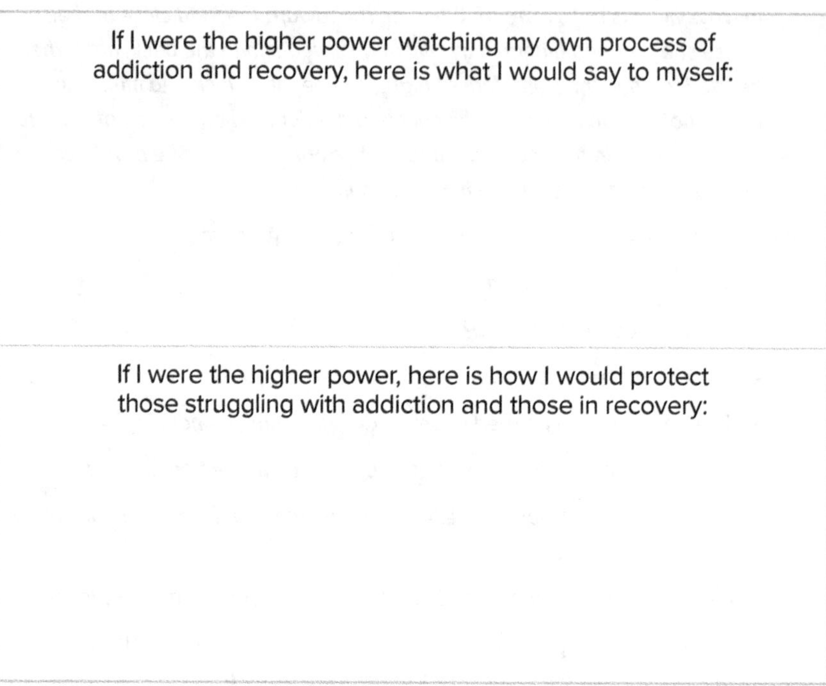

Figure 27

9.   Closing: Leave your client/group with words of encouragement like these:
     *We are all in need of protection. Others can offer us protection. Our higher power
     or purpose can remind us how important we are. Our higher power or purpose can
     become our refuge when recovery is in jeopardy.*

INTERVENTION 21

Bliss in a Box

Addiction takes away many things, often including the ability to care for oneself. Learning or relearning to care for oneself is an important part of recovery. The following intervention will help your client build a custom box of bliss. The box (or bag) should be inexpensive and portable so that it can go wherever your client goes. You may be able to purchase some items at a dollar store, but personal items such as photos of loved ones or favorite places can be more valuable to your client than anything store-bought. The more personalized the box is, the better.

Target Goal: Obtain skills to initiate/maintain sobriety.

Method: Client will develop skills for managing thought, feelings, and situations without substance use.

What you will need: Cardboard box or a drawstring bag, markers (or fabric markers), soothing items to fill the bag (at least one for each of the five senses). Examples: photos of loved ones, perfume samples, stuffed animals, stress ball, coloring pages, markers, healthy snack such as raisin packets.

1. Welcome your client and begin with empathy by asking questions like these:

   - *What made you happy in the last week?*

   - *What was tough?*

   - *What is the most meaningful thing you did in the last week?*

   Listen with care. Highlight the ways in which your client is aware of her experiences, both good and bad. Provide positive feedback for awareness of feelings and point out that it's a sign of progress.

2. Introduce today's task: Building a portable box of bliss to help with self-soothing. You can explain the task like this:

   When we have difficult experiences and feelings it is very easy to get lost in them. The box of bliss will give you an opportunity to step away and help yourself feel a little better by paying attention to your needs and the things and people that are important to you. The box of bliss will not make your difficult experiences and feelings go away, but it will put them in perspective.

3. Review last week's homework. If you assigned a worksheet, ask to see it. Read the worksheet together, or start with a new one. In a group setting, go around the room and ensure that everyone gets an opportunity to reflect on last week's assignment. Always ask specific but open-ended questions. This will help your client find her own answers to questions about sobriety. Telling your client what is good for her can be tempting, but this implies that you do not trust her to find her own path to sobriety. Highlight any successes. If your client completed just a part of the assignment, that is still a success. If she was reluctant to complete the assignment but is able to talk about it, this is also progress, especially if your client has struggled with understanding reluctance in the past.

4. Work on today's task: Give your client a cardboard box or drawstring bag. Explain that it will soon hold things that she can use to comfort herself. Introduce the idea that it is good to use the five senses—sight, hearing, touch, taste, and smell—for self-soothing. Ask your client to reflect on at least one way each of the senses could be used for self-soothing.

5. Ask your client to decorate the box in a way that makes her value herself and is comforting to herself. Be sure to give her enough time to do so. While your client is decorating, ask her questions about the way she is decorating. Here are some questions you may want to ask:

    - *What does the* _________________ (insert item that client is drawing) *mean to you?*

    - *In what way is this item comforting?*

6. Be sure to give positive feedback. Remember, your client is just learning how to express herself again, and perfection is not important. When she finishes, ask about the experience of decorating the box. Was it fun? Did she feel self-conscious about it? Help her recognize and accept any feelings she had while decorating the box.

7. Now it is time to fill the box. Have a selection of items ready. Be creative. A simple item such as a lip balm or lotion can serve as a starting point for self-soothing. Ask your client if she carries any photos that give her comfort. If something is missing, your client can draw it, and you both can look for it between sessions.

8. As you fill the box, ask your client to describe how each item can be used for self-soothing. Make sure you have at least one item for each of the five senses.

9. Summarize: Your client has reflected on the need to self-soothe and created a self-soothing box or bag.

10. Assign homework: Give your client a self-soothing tracking sheet like this and ask her to bring it back to your next meeting:

Bliss Box Tracking			
Item used:	**Date:**	**Result?**	**New ideas:**

Figure 28

11. Closing: Send your client home with words of encouragement like these: *Self-soothing is just like many other things: You have to learn and practice how to do it. This box or bag is a great start. You can add to it to make it better. Being kind to yourself is essential!*

Maintenance

INTERVENTION 22

My Circle

We all live and thrive in relationships. Without meaningful connections to others, we often fail to see meaning and purpose in life. This intervention helps your client explore and understand the importance of being relationally connected. Additionally, this intervention will help your client identify the impact addiction can have on meaningful connections.

This activity is suitable for groups and individual clients.

Stages of Change: Action, maintenance, relapse.

Goal: Reduce the impact of substance use on client functioning and relationships.

Method: Client will gain insight as to how his substance use has impacted his relationships and will work to repair and strengthen healthy relationships.

What you will need: Poster board and marker.

1. Begin with empathy. Welcome your client and ask how the last few days have been. Ask questions like these:

   - *What were your successes over the past few days?*

   - *In what way did you struggle over the past few days?*

   - *When you struggled, what or who helped you?*

   Highlight any successes, no matter how small. Normalize struggles and reinforce the idea that we can make it through difficult times with the help of others.

2. Introduce today's task: Identifying the impact of addiction on your client's circle of support. You can explain the task like this:

   We all need help when things are tough. Our bodies and minds are designed to be relationally connected, to have meaningful friendships and relationships. We need others to support us. Needing others is not a personal flaw; it's part of being human.

3. Review last week's homework: If you assigned a worksheet, ask to see it. Read the worksheet together, or start with a new one. In a group setting, go around the room and ensure that everyone gets an opportunity to reflect on last week's assignment. Always ask specific but open-ended questions. This will help your client find his own answers to questions about sobriety. Telling your client what is good for him can be tempting, but this implies that you do not trust him to find his own path to sobriety. Highlight any successes. If your client completed just a part of the assignment, that is still a success. If he was reluctant to complete the assignment but is able to talk about it, this is also progress, especially if your client has struggled with understanding reluctance in the past.

4. Work on today's task: Take out a poster board and draw the following image:

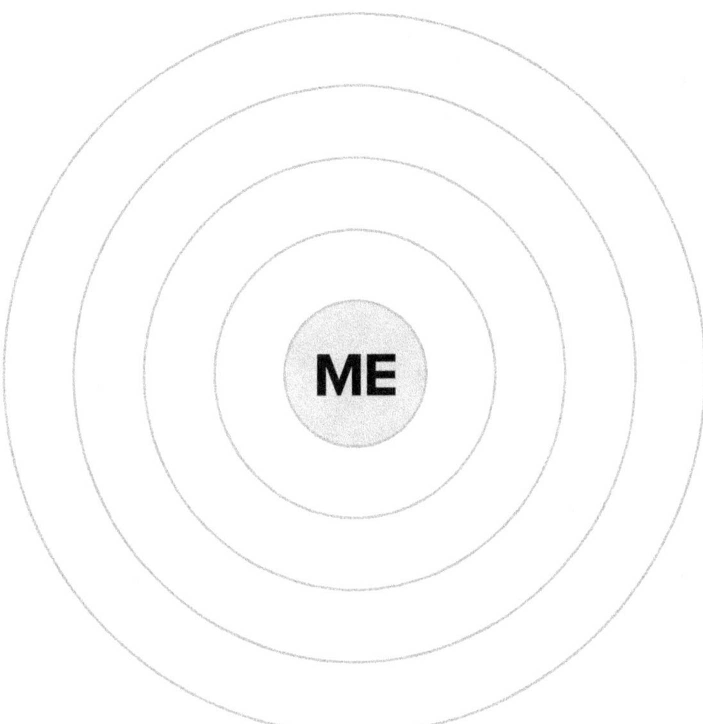

Before my addiction.

Figure 29

5. Ask your client to begin labeling the rings of the circle with the names of loved ones and friends, with those who were closest in the inner circles. Each circle can have more than one name. In a group setting, hand out a worksheet with the image.

   Be sure to give your client or the group enough time to complete the task. Look around to see if anyone has any questions or needs help.

6. Once your client or group members have completed this task, take a look at it together. Explore the circle of human connections your client had before struggling with addiction. Ask:

   - *How did these people support you?*

   - *How did you feel when you were around them?*

   - *In what way did they make your life better?*

7. Repeat the task with a new image, but this time ask your client or group to focus on their circle during addiction. Draw the following image on a poster board.

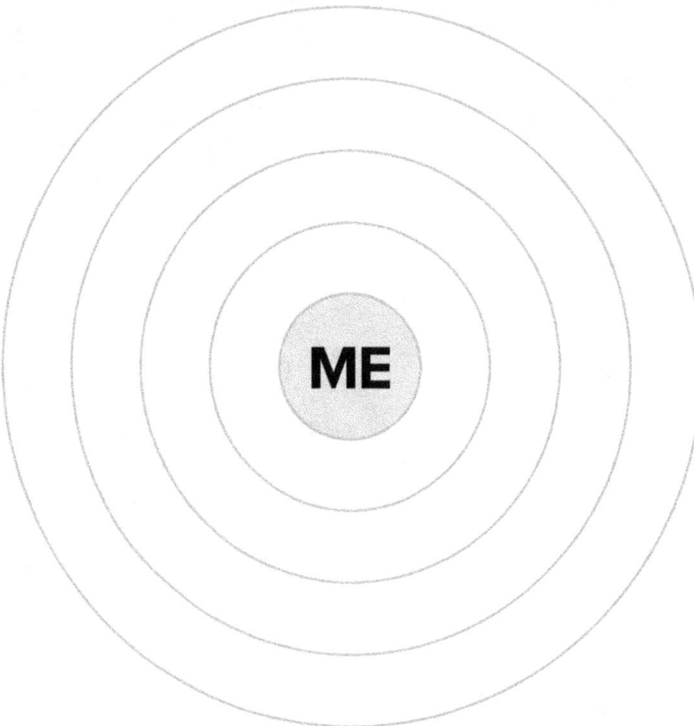

During my addiction.

Figure 30

8. Explore the circle of human connections your client had while in the midst of addiction. Ask:

- *What happened when you were around these people?*
- *How did you feel when you were around them?*
- *Who was no longer part of your circle?*
- *How were you affected by the absence of people you used to be close to?*
- *Who did you miss the most and why?*

Highlight the tendency of addiction to eliminate meaningful connections from our lives and replace them with people who may not have our best interests at heart because they are not capable, at least at that time, of meaningful connection.

9. Lastly, draw another circle like this on the poster board:

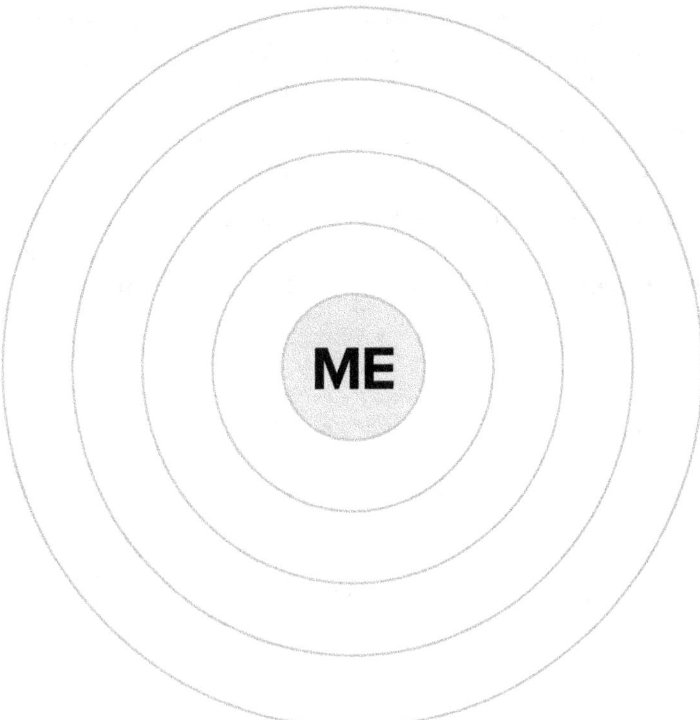

In my recovery.

Figure 31

Ask your client or group to include everyone they want in their lives during recovery and beyond.

If you are using this intervention in a group setting, once again give each group member a worksheet with the above image to complete and be sure to give everyone enough time to complete the task.

10. Then, reflect together. Ask:

   - *Who is back in the circle?*

   - *Why do you want these people back in the circle?*

   - *Who is out?*

   - *Why do you no longer want these people in the circle?*

   - *What do you think can happen once you develop a circle of family and friends like this?*

Elicit specific information about who is back in the circle and who is new in the circle. Pay attention to facial expressions and body language. When you see changes in your client's expression related to this, say things like this:

   - *When you were speaking about* _________________ (enter name of the person in the recovery circle) *I saw your face*_________________ (describe positive facial expression you observed).

- *When you were speaking about* _______________________ (enter name of the person in the recovery circle) *I saw your body*_____________________ (describe positively changed body language you observed).

11. Summarize: Your client has explored circles of connection before and during addiction and begun to design a circle of recovery.

12. Assign homework: Give your client or group the index card below and ask them to pick one person for their circle of recovery. Then ask them to take a concrete step to get back in touch with that person—a phone call, a letter, an email, or a meeting.

The person I want in my recovery circle is:

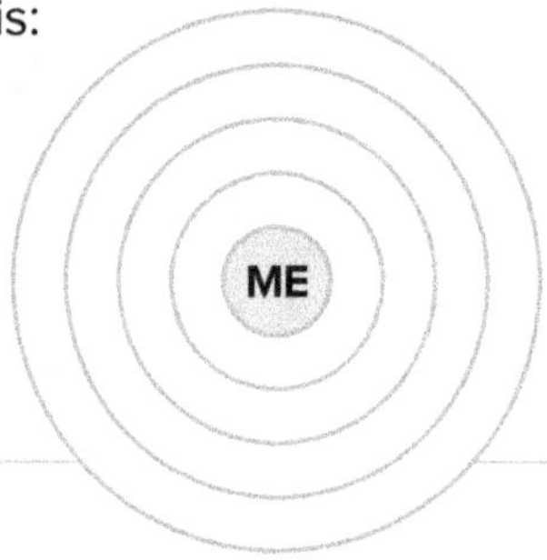

ME

I am going to take this step to connect with this person:

I completed the step above: ☐

Figure 32

Ask them to bring the index card back to the next meeting.

13. Closing: Send your client or group home with words of encouragement like these: *You have in yourself the ability to connect or reconnect with others. These connections can support your recovery. You can take small steps to bring people into your circle of recovery.*

INTERVENTION 23

Letting Go ... 🤍

It's not easy to forgive oneself. We can be harder on ourselves than we are on others. This intervention explores the idea of self-forgiveness. While forgiveness is often described in a religious context, the idea can include spiritual aspects that are nonspecific. Use this intervention in a way that fits your client's needs and values. It's also important to understand that self-condemnation and shame can contribute to relapse.

This activity is suitable for groups and individual clients.

Stages of Change: Action, maintenance, relapse.

Goal: Maintain recovery-oriented behavior changes.

Method: Client will increase knowledge of relapse process, identification of triggers to relapse, and relapse prevention skills.

What you will need: Paper, writing tools, markers, index cards.

1. Begin with empathy. Welcome your client and ask about things and people that are new in her life. Ask questions like these:

    - *What did you do differently in the past few days to support your recovery?*

    - *What kinds of conversations did you have with people who support your recovery?*

    - *What activity or interaction was particularly helpful for your recovery?*

2. Introduce today's task: Learning to look at one's mistakes with kindness and learning to let them go. You can introduce the word *forgiveness,* but only if this is helpful. Here are some things you can say to introduce the task:

    - *When struggling with addiction we often make mistakes. We do things that hurt ourselves and others. When we are in recovery, we may be horrified by some of the things we did and said.*

    - *Yet, being kind to ourselves is one of the most helpful skills in recovery. Today is about cultivating this skill.*

3. Review last week's homework. If you assigned a worksheet, ask to see it. Read the worksheet together, or start with a new one. In a group setting, go around the room and ensure that everyone gets an opportunity to reflect on last week's assignment. Always ask specific but open-ended questions. This will help your client find her own answers to questions about sobriety. Telling your client what is good for her can be tempting, but this implies that you do not trust her to find her own path to sobriety. Highlight any successes. If your client completed just a part of the assignment, that is still a success. If she was reluctant to complete the assignment but is able to talk about it, this is also progress, especially if your client has struggled with understanding reluctance in the past.

4. Work on today's task: Ask your client to listen to a story. Read it with feeling:

There once was a wonderful child. The child was full of life and had an amazing ability to play and learn. The child's parents enjoyed the child, and the child enjoyed his parents. As the child got older, a dark cloud seemed to descend on him. He was often withdrawn and sad, irritable and angry. When he was irritable and angry he said terrible things to his mother and father. Sometimes he pushed or hit them. He was no longer a good friend to his playmates. He was mean to them, and they quit inviting him to play dates. Now the child was also lonely. This made things only worse.

Finally, someone saw that the child was not well, and the child got help. Gradually things got better. The child and his parents learned that the boy had been struggling with depression. With treatment the child got better. He now felt awful about the terrible things he had said and done to his parents and playmates. He wanted to punish himself for what he did and began telling himself what an awful person he is.

5. Pause and ask your client or group to take a deep breath together. Then ask them to put themselves in the child's parents' shoes and come up with at least three helpful responses to the child's desire to punish himself and his condemnation of himself. Give everyone an index card and pen. In a group setting, you can also pair up people to work on responses together. Ask your client or group members to write the responses on an index card.

6. After about ten minutes, ask your client or group to share their responses. Highlight any that include kind words and point in the direction of forgiveness.

7. Then ask:

   - *Why do you think you, as the parent, were kind to the child?*

   - *Why are you not encouraging the child to punish himself?*

   - *What do you want to achieve by being kind to the child?*

   Highlight any responses that put the child's behavior into the context of his illness and help him learn that forgiveness is possible.

8. Help your client or group make the connection between their struggles with the illness of addiction and the child's struggles by asking:

   - *In what ways did addiction make it difficult for you to be kind to others and yourself?*

   - *In what ways did addiction make you do and say things that you now consider wrong or mean?*

   Listen and highlight responses that illustrate the connection between the illness of addiction and words and behaviors that were harmful to others or oneself.

9. Ask your client or group members to pick up the index card of the response they would give to the child in the story. Ask your client to share a self-condemning and punishing thought. Borrow his index card with kind and helpful words for the child, and read those words to your client with feeling

and conviction. In a group setting, ask members to pair up and take turns with sharing condemning and punishing thoughts, then listening to the words they wrote on the index cards.

10. Pause and ask how it feels to receive those kind words. Highlight acceptance of any part of the helpful and kind statements. Explain that kindness to oneself and forgiveness for past mistakes is a skill that is learned over time. Explain that addiction often tells us that what we have said and done is unforgivable, but that this is simply not true.

11. Summarize: You have explored the idea of letting go, of being kind and forgiving oneself through the story of a child who said and did hurtful things. You have practiced accepting kind and helpful words.

12. Assign homework: Send the index card with the three kind and helpful things home with your client or group. Ask them to end every day by reading the index card aloud. Suggest keeping the index card on the nightstand or another place close by, as this can increase homework completion.

13. Closing: Send your client home with words of encouragement like these:

    Kindness to oneself can be learned. When we learn to forgive ourselves for things we said and did in the midst of addiction, those things can cease to be triggers for relapse. Forgiving and being kind to oneself is a skill learned step by step. Take this one day at a time.

INTERVENTION 24

Beyond Me

Addiction is an illness that affects more than just the person struggling with it. Addiction affects families and friends. When addiction takes hold, it does not leave voluntarily. Breaking the chains of addiction can positively impact many people in the present and in the future. This intervention is designed for those who have built a solid foundation of recovery and are able to explore the positive impact they can now have.

This activity is suitable for groups and individual clients.

Stages of Change: Action, maintenance.

Goal: Maintain recovery-oriented behavior changes.

Method: Client will gain insight as to how substance use has impacted relationships and will work to repair and strengthen healthy relationships.

What you will need: Paper, writing tools, markers, index cards, poster board.

1. Begin with empathy.Welcome your client or group by saying: *I am so glad you are here. You have come so far. You can be proud of fighting for your sobriety every day.*

2. Introduce today's task: Exploring the impact of sobriety and recovery on oneself, those around us, and even those who come after us. You can say: *When we become sober, our lives become richer. Over time, we gain clarity. We reconnect and build new connections. These connections affect us and those around us.*

3. Review last week's homework: If you assigned a worksheet, ask to see it. Read the worksheet together, or start with a new one. In a group setting, go around the room and ensure that everyone gets an opportunity to reflect on last week's assignment. Always ask specific but open-ended questions. This will help your client find his own answers to questions about sobriety. Telling your client what is good for him can be tempting, but this implies that you do not trust him to find his own path to sobriety. Highlight any successes. If your client completed just a part of the assignment, that is still a success. If he was reluctant to complete the assignment but is able to talk about it, this is also progress, especially if your client has struggled with understanding reluctance in the past.

4. Work on today's task: On a poster board or worksheet, present the Beyond Me chain image.

Figure 33

5. Ask your client or group members to share a vivid story about how recovery has impacted them positively. Ask for details. Here are some sample questions you can ask:

   - *What positive thing happened in your life that would not have happened if you were not in recovery?*
   - *Where were you when this thing happened?*
   - *Who was with you?*
   - *How did you feel?*

   The goal is not only to learn about your client's new positive experiences related to recovery but also to invoke the positive emotions this experience brought up; in other words, to relive the moment in the present. In a group setting, write the questions on a poster board and pair up group members so they can ask each other, then report to the group.

6. Ask your client or group to write the name of the person closest to them on the poster board or worksheet. Then ask them to explain in detail how recovery has positively affected this person. Ask for a specific situation. You can ask:

   - *How do you know that this person benefits from your recovery?*
   - *What are you now doing together that you did not use to do?*
   - *What has this person said to you that makes it clear they benefit from your recovery?*
   - *How do you feel when you think about the specific situation you described?*
   - *What do you think will happen in the future because the two of you are now connected again, thanks to you being in recovery?*

7. Ask your client or group to name at least three other people who are positively affected by their recovery. They can include children! You can repeat the questions in the previous step. In a group setting, write the questions on a poster board and pair up group members so they can ask each other, then report to the group.

8. Summarize: You have explored how recovery positively impacts not only the person in recovery but also those around them. Explain that each person in recovery can be proud about changing not only their own life but also others' lives. Explain that a relapse does not erase positive experiences related to recovery. Those experiences are real and still count.

9. Assign homework. Give your client/group members the following index card to complete and bring back to your next meeting:

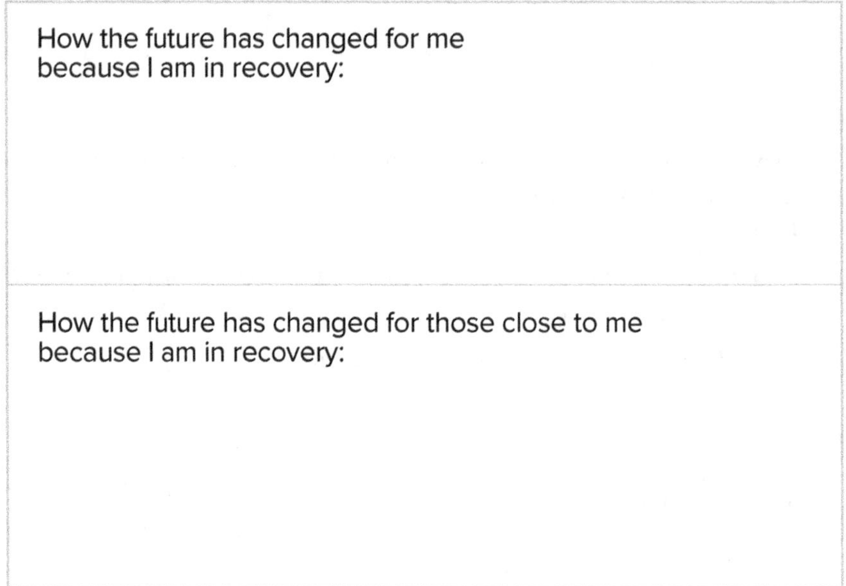

Figure 34

10. Closing: Send your client or group home with words of encouragement like these: *You are now changing lives for the better. These positive changes can affect generations to come. Your sobriety matters.*

INTERVENTION 25

Staying Connected 💜

People in recovery often have strong attachments to friends who are still suffering from active addiction and may feel an urgency to help them. This may put their own recovery in jeopardy as they may want to stay in touch with these friends and support them, perhaps with money or in other ways. This creates risk for the person in recovery. Turning away from those in active addiction can feel like abandoning them. This intervention explores how those in recovery can stay connected with those in active addiction without jeopardizing their own recovery, using mindfulness exercises or prayers. This intervention is for clients who are open to exploring the role of a higher power or purpose in their recovery.

This activity is suitable for groups and individual clients.

Stages of Change: Action, maintenance.

Goal: Reduce risk of relapse.

Method: Client will learn refusal skills, decrease association with other substance users, and increase associations with sober supports.

What you will need: Paper, writing tools, markers, index cards, poster board, small basket, small zip-lock baggies.

1. Welcome your client and begin with empathy. You can say:

    - *I am so happy that you are here.*

    - *Every sober day counts.*

    - *I am proud of the steps you have taken to become sober and maintain your recovery.*

2. Introduce today's task: Staying connected with those dear to us who are still struggling with active addiction. You can explain:

    It's human to want to stay connected. We all have friends who are still struggling with addiction. Because we are good people, we want to help them. But we have to do this in ways that do not put our sobriety at risk. This is what today is about.

3. Review last week's homework. If you assigned a worksheet, ask to see it. Read the worksheet together, or start with a new one. In a group setting, go around the room and ensure that everyone gets an opportunity to reflect on last week's assignment. Always ask specific but open-ended questions. This will help your client find her own answers to questions about sobriety. Telling your client what is good for her can be tempting, but this implies that you do not trust her to find her own path to sobriety. Highlight any successes. If your client completed just a part of the assignment, that is still a success. If she was reluctant to complete the assignment but is able to talk about it, this is also progress, especially if your client has struggled with understanding reluctance in the past.

4. Work on today's task: Ask your client or group to tell you about one person who is important to them and still struggling with active addiction. Ask them:

    - how they feel when they talk about this person now.
    - about positive experiences they had with this person, even if these experiences took place in the context of addiction.
    - about hopes and fears for this person.

5. Highlight the words related to feelings and connections that they use. Ask how they have tried to help the person still struggling with addiction.

6. Using a worksheet (with an individual client) or poster board (in a group setting), explore the implications of helping the person still in active addiction using this chart:

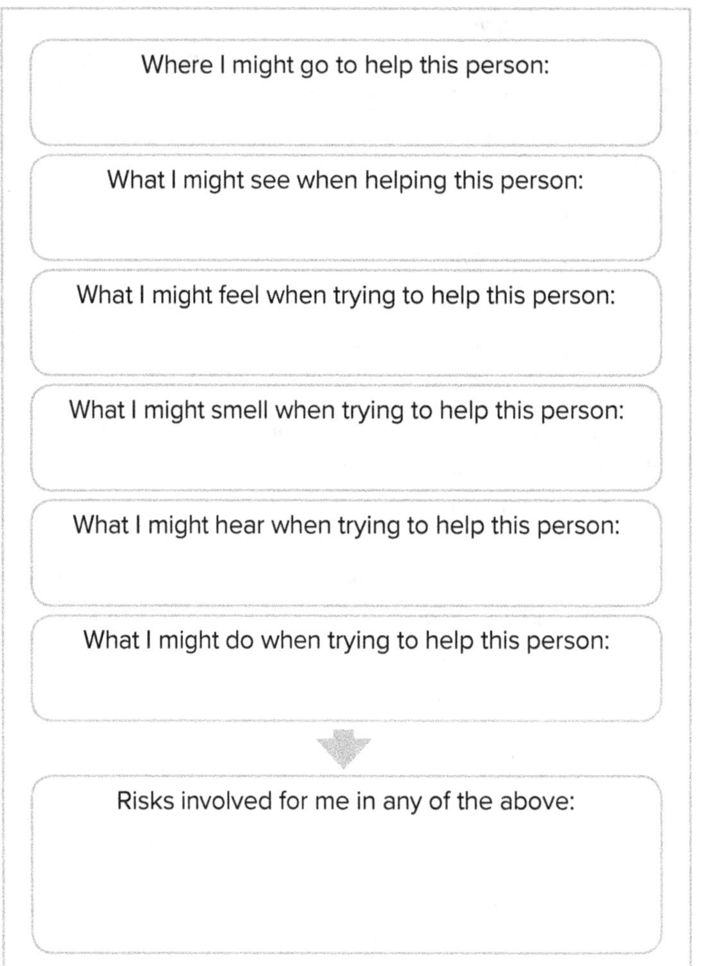

Figure 35

7. Help your client or group balance their need to help those who are still struggling with addiction with their need to stay in recovery. Say:

   Helping others is a noble thing. The fact that you want to help this person speaks to your loving and compassionate nature. But you won't be able to help your friend if you relapse. You are helping your friend simply by staying sober—it shows that staying sober can be done with the right support and in the right environment.

8. Listen for concerns. Reiterate how kind it is to want to help, but also ask open-ended questions about risks involved in helping.

9. Introduce the idea of mindful presence with those who are still in active addiction. Explain that there are many ways to help, such as:

   - contributing to an organization that helps those in active addiction through volunteering time or donating items;

   - being living examples of the road to recovery; and

   - sending mindful thoughts into the world or sending prayers to our higher power or purpose.

10. Summarize: You have explored ways, though well intentioned, in which connections with those still struggling with active addiction could put your own recovery at risk. You have introduced the idea that there are many ways to help old friends, such as mindful thoughts and prayers.

11. Assign homework: Ask your client or group to write a prayer or wish for their old friends and ask for the presence of the divine or all that is good in the world with the old friend, even in the midst of addiction. Ask that your client/group members write this on an index card (hand out index cards) and bring it to your next meeting.

12. Closing: Send your client or group home with words of encouragement like these: *You are on the right path! There are many ways to support others. Pick those that are safe for you and will keep you on the right path.*

INTERVENTION 26

Blooming

This intervention uses the metaphor of a blooming flower to help clients understand how beautiful sobriety is. Of course, flowers need to be watered, just as sobriety has to be tended to every day. This is a hands-on intervention: Your client or group will walk home with a flower to remind them of the beauty of sobriety.

This activity is suitable for groups and individual clients.

Stages of Change: Action, maintenance.

Goal: Reduce risk of relapse.

Method: Client will develop alternative coping skills and implement them to manage stressors and triggers.

What you will need: Paper, writing tools, markers, glue stick, scissors.

1. Welcome your client and begin with empathy by saying things like this:

   - *I have watched you grow and become more secure in your sobriety. It's a beautiful thing to see.*

   - *You have built a support network for your sobriety. Well done.*

   Pay attention to your client's or group members' nonverbal responses. If you see a face relax or a smile develop, point this out and remind them of the value of the work they are doing.

2. Introduce today's task: Recognizing the beauty of sobriety and its impact in all areas of life. You can say: *Sobriety is like a beautiful flower. It grows over time. It needs care to grow. Just like a flower has many petals, sobriety has many elements.*

3. Review last week's homework: If you assigned a worksheet, ask to see it. Read the worksheet together, or start with a new one. In a group setting, go around the room and ensure that everyone gets an opportunity to reflect on last week's assignment. Always ask specific but open-ended questions. This will help your client find his own answers to questions about sobriety. Telling your client what is good for him can be tempting, but this implies that you do not trust him to find his own path to sobriety. Highlight any successes. If your client completed just a part of the assignment, that is still a success. If he was reluctant to complete the assignment but is able to talk about it, this is also progress, especially if your client has struggled with understanding reluctance in the past.

4. Work on today's task: Give your client the following worksheet with a flower stem, petals, center.

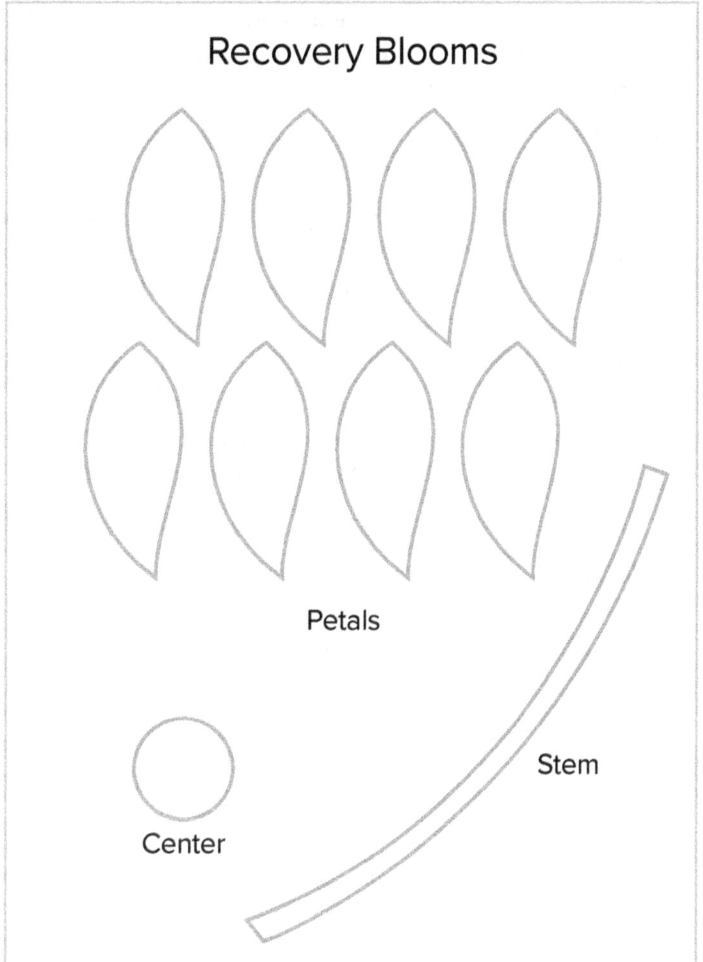

Figure 36

Ask your client or group to color, cut out, and assemble the piece of the flower and glue them to another sheet of paper. This should take about 10 minutes or so.

5. Once the flowers are glued down, ask:

    - *How do you feel when you look at this beautiful flower?*

    - *What is your favorite thing about it?*

    - *In what way is your sobriety like this beautiful flower?*

    - *What have you done to make the flower grow?*

    - *What will you need to continue to do?*

Listen and highlight that both plants and sobriety need regular care. If your client is critical of his flower, help him find the beauty of what he has created and then draw parallels to sobriety. Sobriety is beautiful in itself. Sobriety does not have to look like a rose. It's still a flower, even if it is a wildflower.

6.   Ask your client to identify one element of sobriety that is beautiful for each petal. It could be something like a new friend, the ability to learn again, or just experiencing the world fully again.

7.   Summarize: You have explored ways in which sobriety is like a beautiful flower and have identified elements of beauty in sobriety.

8.   Assign homework: Send the flower image and an index card home with your client or group. Ask them to hang up the image in prominent place, perhaps close to their bed, and to look at it at the end of every day. On the index card, they should identify at least one way in which they "watered" the flower of sobriety that day. Have them bring the index card back to your next meeting.

9.   Closing: Send your client or group home with words of encouragement like: *You have the capacity to create something beautiful. No matter how small, a flower is still a flower and no matter how precarious, sobriety is still sobriety.*

Relapse Prevention

Lapse vs. Relapse

Moving toward recovery is a wonderful thing. It can also be difficult, and some form of relapse is to be expected. But not every lapse constitutes a full-blown relapse. When your client lapses (using a substance once without significant consequences), it is important to frame this as an opportunity rather than a failure. Clearly something led to the lapse. Perhaps a coping skill was not working, or an unexpected life circumstance occurred. What does this mean for your client's recovery? You can use the following image to help your client understand the difference between a lapse and a relapse:

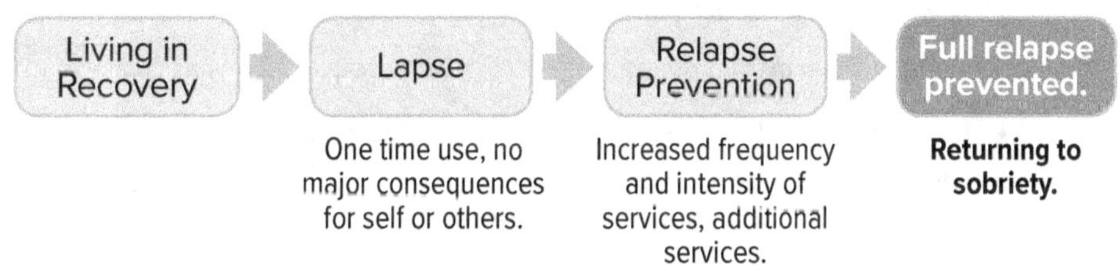

Figure 37

When a lapse occurs, your client may need increased frequency, intensity, or variety of services; further assessment; or an amended relapse prevention plan. In other words, more and better planning is needed. You and your client should explore, in depth, what led to the lapse. Perhaps your client needs to increase the frequency of twelve-step meetings or remove herself from people who offer her substances. You may also discover that an underlying mental health condition needs treatment. All these things should be addressed clearly and added to your client's treatment plan. If your client does not yet have a peer recovery support worker, refer her for this service. Those with lived experience may be better able to relate to your client's struggles with staying sober and building a sober support system.

Provide positive feedback for bringing the lapse to your attention. Of course, you will also need to make sure that your client is not minimizing her use. Find out if the lapse was really a relapse, meaning that your client used substances more than once, and there were negative consequences for her or someone else. Do so without shaming or blaming. Ask open-ended questions about her use and let her tell you if she has experienced a one-time lapse or a relapse.

How I Got There...

When relapse occurs, it is important for your client to understand what happened. There could be more than one contributing factor or action. It can be easy to attribute a relapse, prematurely, to one event or action when really it was a series of circumstances. This intervention will help your client, who is committed to recovery but has hit a snag and relapsed, better explore and understand events and actions that lead it so that another relapse can be anticipated and prevented.

This activity is suitable for groups and individual clients.

Stages of Change: Action, maintenance, relapse.

Goal: Reduce risk of relapse.

Method: Client will increase knowledge of relapse process, identification of triggers to relapse, and relapse prevention skills.

What you will need: White board and white board marker or large piece of paper and colorful markers.

1. Welcome your client and begin with empathy. Ask about the past week to connect with his experiences. You can ask:

   - *Who did you meet up with this week?*

   - *Who did you miss this week?*

   - *What did you do that gave you a sense of purpose and belonging?*

   In a group setting, give every member a chance to respond.

2. Introduce today's task: Understanding relapse, including actions and events that lead up to it and related triggers. Briefly provide psychoeducation about relapse as part of recovery. You can say:

   Think of addiction in the way that you think of other illnesses, such as high blood pressure or diabetes. When you have high blood pressure or diabetes, you have to take care of this illness every day. You have to follow your doctor's orders and treatment recommendations in order to be well. Addiction is very much the same. Addiction requires ongoing, daily maintenance. When you have diabetes, you may have to take medication and follow a specific diet. Still, diabetes can act up. Addiction is similar to this. Sometimes, relapse can happen.

3. Review last week's homework: If you asked your client to complete a worksheet, take a look at it together. Ask questions about his answers and highlight any steps he took to maintain sobriety. If your client relapsed, help him focus on understanding that this is a part of the process of recovery.

4. Work on today's task: Ask your client to recall his last relapse. In a group setting, ask for a volunteer. Remind everyone that the group is a safe and judgment-free zone. It's not OK to shame a group member because he relapsed.

5. On a large piece of paper or white board, draw a long, horizontal line. You will use this line as a timeline.

6. Ask your client when the relapse occurred and mark it about halfway on the line like this:

Figure 38

Ask your client for specific (but non-gory) details about the relapse. Then ask if any important life events occurred days or weeks before, such as a divorce, death, job loss, or perceived rejection. Mark all those events on the timeline. At this time, discourage your client and group members from drawing conclusions about what led to the relapse.

7. Use Socratic questions to help your client or group make connections and draw conclusions. For example:

   - *How did you feel after you lost your job?*

   - *When your friends walked away from you, how did you manage the loss?*

   - *How much support did you have when your partner filed for divorce?*

   If necessary, reiterate the need to stay away from judgment. This intervention is not about shame or blame; it is about understanding and prevention.

8. Use colored markers to help your client make connections between events, actions, and triggers. Ask if your or other group members' inferences are accurate.

9. Based on the timeline, create a list of the triggers and social, emotional, physical, environmental, and behavioral factors that led to relapse.

10. Summarize: Your client has explored events that occurred prior to a relapse. He has then created a list of factors that can contribute to a relapse. The list is specific to him—which makes it a much more useful list.

11. Assign homework: Send your client home with the following relapse prevention worksheet:

Factors that can contribute to relapse:	Things I can do to address these factors:
Social:	
Emotional:	
Physical:	
Environmental:	
Behavioral:	
General Triggers:	

Figure 39

12. Ask your client to bring this rudimentary relapse prevention plan to your next meeting.

13. Closing: Send your client home with words of encouragement. In a group setting, ask everyone to offer encouragement to the person to their left. If you need to, you can give examples like these:

- *You have come so far.*
- *You can be proud of yourself.*
- *It means a lot that you come here.*
- *It's great to have your support and to support you.*

INTERVENTION 28

The Planet of Recovery

This intervention links with the Planet of Addiction intervention, but it can also stand alone. Recovery, too, can be a strange planet for those who have struggled with addiction. Your client's memories of life before addiction may be faint. Addiction's pull is so strong that living in recovery can seem like living on a new and unfamiliar planet that has to be mapped and explored.

This activity is suitable for groups and individual clients.

Stages of Change: Contemplation, action, maintenance, relapse.

Goal: Increase awareness of addiction to increase motivation for recovery-oriented change.

Method: Client will develop skills to manage thoughts, feelings, and situations without substance use.

What you will need: Paper, writing tools, markers, index cards.

1. Begin with empathy. Ask your client or group about the last week. You can ask:

   - *What experiences pointed you in the direction of recovery?*

   - *What interactions pointed you in the direction of recovery?*

   Highlight any positive experiences and interactions, no matter how small. It is important that your client find in herself the ability to move toward recovery.

2. Identify today's task: Exploring and inhabiting the planet of recovery. You can say this to help everyone understand the task:

   Recovery is a great place to walk toward. Think of recovery as a planet you once knew—before addiction took over. Think of recovery also as a planet you are getting to know—it is different now that you have lived with active addiction. You may need a whole new roadmap. Things that used to be familiar may now seem strange.

3. Review last week's homework: If you assigned a worksheet, ask to see it. Read the worksheet together, or start with a new one. In a group setting, go around the room and ensure that everyone gets an opportunity to reflect on last week's assignment. Always ask specific but open-ended questions. This will help your client find her own answers to questions about sobriety. Telling your client what is good for her can be tempting, but this implies that you do not trust her to find her own path to sobriety. Highlight any successes. If your client completed just a part of the assignment, that is still a success. If she was reluctant to complete the assignment but is able to talk about it, this is also progress, especially if your client has struggled with understanding reluctance in the past.

4. Work on today's task: Hang the poster board and draw the following image:

Figure 40

5. Ask your client or group to name familiar elements on the planet of recovery. Write those on the image of the planet.

6. Next, ask your client or group to name the unfamiliar elements. Write those on the image of the planet.

7. Help your client or group explore and understand how familiar and unfamiliar elements come together to form the planet of recovery by asking questions like these:

   - *How do the things you know about on the planet of recovery relate to the things that seem unfamiliar?*

   - *Which things do you welcome with open arms?*

   - *Which are you unsure about or afraid of?*

   - *What is different about this planet that may make it easier to deal with the things you are unsure about or afraid of?*

   Highlight any responses that emphasize human connections.

8. Ask:

   - *Who is with you on this planet?*

   - *In what way are those who are with you helping you to walk toward recovery?*

   - *What is it like to have meaningful and supportive relationships again?*

   - *How have you found yourself able to be helpful to others?*

9. Summarize: You have explored the realities, including hopes and fears, on the planet of recovery. You have identified together that the planet of recov-

ery is characterized by regained and newly built connections and that it is those connections that make it possible to face things that provoke anxiety.

10. Assign homework: Give your client or group the following index card to complete and bring back to your next meeting:

The ideal planet of recovery has:

1. _______________________________________

2. _______________________________________

3. _______________________________________

4. _______________________________________

5. _______________________________________

Figure 41

11. Closing: Send your client or group home with words of encouragement like these: *Exploring the planet of recovery is exciting. So many new and old things to discover. It can also be a bit frightening. New things are both exciting and a bit scary. It's OK to feel this way. Every new thing on this planet is an opportunity to build your recovery!*

INTERVENTION 29

Cry for Help 🖤

To cry for help in times of distress is human. Those struggling with addiction may find themselves in distress frequently because they themselves or others around them are in danger. It's human to send a prayer for help into the world. This intervention is designed to help your client explore and reflect on his interactions with his higher power or purpose. This intervention is not for those who reject the idea of a higher power or purpose, even when broadly defined.

This activity is suitable for groups and individual clients.

Stages of Change: Action, maintenance.

Goal: Reduce risk of relapse.

Method: Client will develop alternative coping skills and implement them to manage stressors and triggers.

What you will need: Paper, writing tools, markers, index cards, poster board, small basket, small zip-lock baggies.

1. Welcome your client and begin with empathy. Ask about your client's feelings and overall mood. Reflect back his feelings and express support. You can say: *Bad moods are a burden. They seem so heavy. I am here to support you. Even if I can't fix the situation, I am here for you.*

2. Introduce today's task: Exploring our relationship with a higher power or purpose and how addiction and recovery may affect this relationship. You can explain it like this:

   - *We often cry out to our higher power when we are in trouble. What kind of response are we hoping for?*

   - *When things get better, we may forget about our higher power or purpose.*

3. Review last week's homework. If you assigned a worksheet, ask to see it. Read the worksheet together, or start with a new one. In a group setting, go around the room and ensure that everyone gets an opportunity to reflect on last week's assignment. Always ask specific but open-ended questions. This will help your client find his own answers to questions about sobriety. Telling your client what is good for him can be tempting, but this implies that you do not trust him to find his own path to sobriety. Highlight any successes. If your client completed just a part of the assignment, that is still a success. If he was reluctant to complete the assignment but is able to talk about it, this is also progress, especially if your client has struggled with understanding reluctance in the past.

4. Work on today's task: Give your client or group the following worksheet to complete. If you are using this intervention in a group setting, give everyone the worksheet and at least ten minutes to complete the task. If your client struggles with writing, he can draw instead, or you or another group member can serve as a scribe.

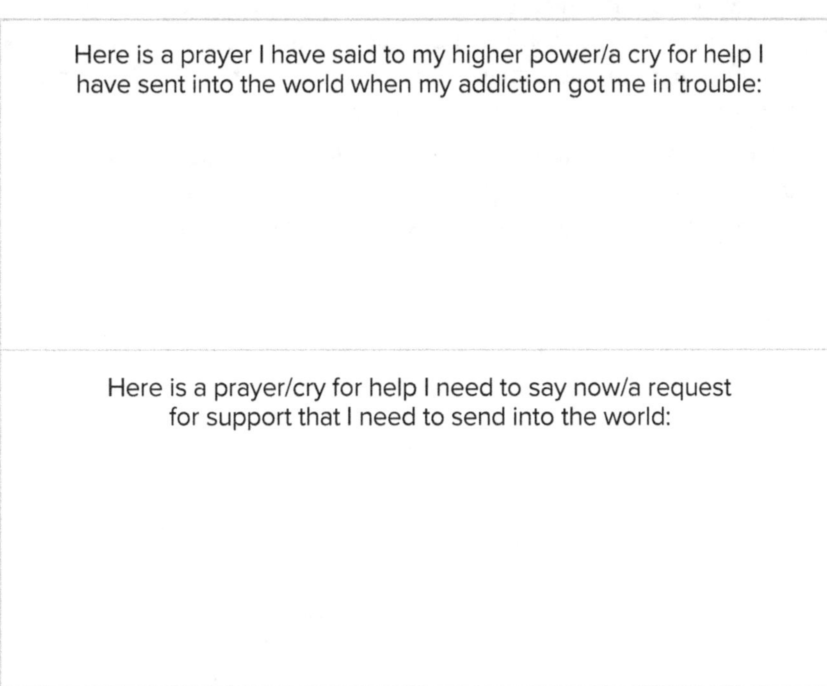

Figure 42

5. Look around. When most everyone or your client is done, prompt your client or group members to share their responses. Remind everyone to be respectful. Prayers can be very personal. Explain that sharing is voluntary and let those who do not wish to share do so.

6. Validate the expressed need for support and divine intervention. Addiction feels so monstrous that asking for divine intervention is common even among those who don't usually pray.

7. Ask your client how prayer or meditation can be helpful in recovery. You can ask:

    - *What if you dedicated five minutes at the beginning of each day to building your connection with your higher power or purpose?*

    - *What do you think would be the impact on your recovery?*

    - *What would happen if you expanded this to dedicate five minutes at the beginning and end of every day?*

    - *What would happen if you reflected on your connection with your higher power or purpose regularly, not just when you are in extreme distress?*

8. Summarize: You have explored how addiction can lead to an urgent need to connect with one's higher power or purpose. Your client has explored this connection and how it could support recovery.

9. Assign homework: Give your client five index cards. Ask him to record at least three short prayers or requests for the universe in the next few days and bring them to your next meeting. You may want to put the index cards in small zip-lock baggies so that they do not get lost.

10. Closing: Send your client home with words of encouragement like these: *You are connected with all those who support you and your higher power or purpose. This is true even when you do not think of it. It does not change.*

INTERVENTION 30

Risky Business

This intervention is designed to help your client explore and understand the draw of high-risk situations, such as visiting people or places associated with drug use. In order to prevent a relapse, it is necessary to understand why we may be drawn to those situations.

This activity is suitable for groups and individual clients.

Stages of Change: Relapse.

Goal: Obtain skills to maintain sobriety.

Method: Client will increase knowledge of relapse process, identification of triggers to relapse, and relapse prevention skills.

What you will need: Paper and markers.

1. Welcome your client and begin with empathy. Say something like this:

    - *You have some so far. You can be proud of yourself.*

    - *Others are noticing your hard work.*

    - *You are reaping the benefits of sobriety.*

2. Introduce today's task: Exploring and understanding the pull into high-risk situations that carry the risk of relapsing. You can say:

    I understand that you are committed to sobriety, and you are beginning to feel more secure in your sobriety. Maybe even so secure that you feel like it's OK to visit old friends who are still using and places you used to hang out and use. But people, places, and things that are associated with addiction can have a strong pull that can't be rationally explained. Relapse prevention means identifying, understanding, and respecting what may trigger a relapse, even when you think it won't.

3. Review last week's homework: If you assigned a worksheet, ask to see it. Read the worksheet together, or start with a new one. In a group setting, go around the room and ensure that everyone gets an opportunity to reflect on the assignment. Always ask specific but open-ended questions. This will help your clients find their own answers to questions about sobriety. Telling them what is good for them can be tempting, but it implies that you do not trust them to find their own path. Highlight any successes. If a client completed just a part of the assignment, that is still a success. If the client was reluctant to complete the assignment but is able to talk about it, this is also progress, especially if that client has struggled with understanding reluctance in the past.

4. Work on today's task: Give your client or group five pieces of paper and markers and ask them to write or draw at least five people, places, and things that could trigger a relapse. Explain that often triggers can "live" in the same environment. For example:

Ronald goes to check on his old friend Lee, who is still struggling with active addiction. Lee often buys drugs from Ron's old dealer. When Ron sees Lee, he feels strangely triggered to use again and does not fully understand why. It's just happening.

Explain that this activity may best be completed by just writing or drawing whatever immediately comes to mind. Offer more paper to anyone who needs it.

5. Ask the following questions to help your client or group reflect:

    - *Which triggers did you come up with?*

    - *Which triggers do you think you can now easily handle?*

    - *Which may be harder to manage?*

    - *What makes you think you can manage a specific trigger?*

    - *What would happen if you were wrong about your ability to manage the trigger?*

    - *In what ways has addiction tricked you in the past about being able to handle substances?*

    - *How might addiction be attempting to trick you now?*

    - *What are valid reasons for not moving toward triggers even if you think you can handle them?*

    Highlight any responses that express an understanding of the traps that addiction sets by making us believe that we can handle things that we can't. Explain that not being able to handle a trigger is not a weakness, and that recognizing the triggers that can make us feel powerless against addiction is a sign of progressing recovery. You can say:

    Once you accept that triggers have immense power, you can make choices based on that understanding. These choices keep you on the road to recovery.

6. Give your client the following worksheet to complete:

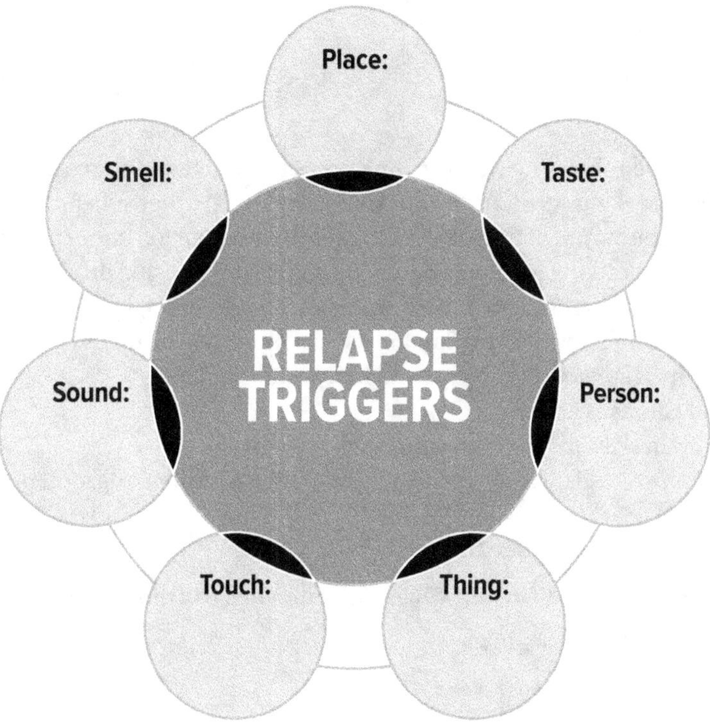

Figure 43

This trigger identification worksheet is a work in progress. You can add to it over time.

7. Summarize: You have explored thoughts about relapse triggers. You have begun to explore that some triggers may seem manageable but should be avoided. You have created a relapse trigger reminder worksheet.

8. Assign homework: Ask your client or group to take the relapse trigger worksheet home and identify at least one alternative to each situation; for example, spending time with sober friends instead of visiting one still struggling with active addiction or visiting a favorite bar. Ask your client to be very specific when identifying alternatives, including names and phone numbers. Explain that when triggers attempt to trick us, it is hard to think clearly, so it's best to be prepared to avoid them.

9. Send your client home with words of encouragement like these: *You can manage triggers by avoiding them. You can make plans to have a life away from triggers. When triggers call, you can have sober friends around you to help.*

INTERVENTION 31

The Media

Addiction often shows up in our online presence. Interactions on social media become about seeking substances and connections with other substance users, leaving our accounts full of triggers. Old friends may be talking about using or obtaining drugs or trying to make connections that lead to using drugs. Those who are in recovery may want to help those still in active addiction, but this can lead to relapse. Your client may need to plan for a social media clean-up or restart.

This activity is suitable for groups and individual clients.

Stages of Change: Action.

Goal: Obtain skills to maintain sobriety.

Method: Client will increase communication, decision-making, and problem-solving skills.

What you will need: Paper and markers.

1. Welcome your client and begin with empathy. Say things like this:

    - *You have come so far.*

    - *You are no longer alone.*

    - *You are in recovery together with others.*

2. Introduce today's task: Managing social media accounts, contacts, and interactions.

3. Review last week's homework. If you assigned a worksheet, ask to see it. Read the worksheet together, or start with a new one. In a group setting, go around the room and ensure that everyone gets an opportunity to reflect on the assignment. Always ask specific but open-ended questions. This will help your clients find their own answers to questions about sobriety. Telling them what is good for them can be tempting, but it implies that you do not trust them to find their own path. Highlight any successes. If a client completed just a part of the assignment, that is still a success. If the client was reluctant to complete the assignment but is able to talk about it, this is also progress, especially if that client has struggled with understanding reluctance in the past.

4. Work on today's task: Exploring past use of social media accounts and their relationship to addiction, and making a plan to use those accounts to further recovery and sobriety for oneself and others. Give your client or group the following image and ask them to write about or draw people, places, and things related to drug use:

The Book of Faces
Instapost and the Like.

Drug-related posts:

Figure 44

5. Help your client or group to explore how they felt about this. Ask:

    - *What did it feel like to draw or write about this world?*

    - *What or who do your miss from that world?*

    - *In what ways were you triggered to wanting substances while you were drawing or writing?*

    Validate any losses. It's quite possible that your client or group will miss aspects of their past. It's OK to acknowledge that choosing sobriety means giving up things that we miss.

6. Give new copies of the image, but this time ask your client or group to write about or draw aspects of a sober life. Ask them to be as specific as possible. Then take a look together and ask:

    - *What do you see?*

    - *Who is on your page with you?*

    - *What are you talking about on your page?*

    - *What pictures are you posting?*

    - *How would you feel after looking at this page?*

    - *In what way does this page now move you forward in your recovery?*

    Highlight any responses that signal change, such as the willingness to make new sober friends and unfriending a former drug dealer.

7. Summarize: You have explored how your client used social media accounts while struggling with active addiction, and how those accounts now can reflect a commitment to sobriety.

8. Assign homework: Give your client or group the following worksheet and ask them to identify at least three things they need to do in order to clean up current social media accounts to decrease the risk of relapse. Ask them to bring the worksheet back to your next meeting.

The Book of Faces
Instapost and the Like.

Things I need to do to make my social
media accounts sobriety-building:

1. ____

2. ____

3. ____

4. ____

5. ____

Figure 45

9. Send your client home with words of encouragement like this: *You are building safe and sober connections here. It's possible also to do this on social media. Safe and sober online connections will move you further in your recovery.*

SUD Targeted Case Management Interventions

SUD targeted case management interventions are often, but not always, delivered by nonlicensed mental health providers, such as peer support specialists. Licensed mental health providers can provide these interventions. However, if a client requires a lot of case management support, the client should be referred to a nonlicensed provider in order to streamline service delivery.

In the context of SUD services, case management interventions often center around managing basic needs. It's a lot harder to become sober when you are homeless, can't afford to eat, and are isolated and unemployed. Meeting basic needs is critical. It's also a great way to connect with a client who is struggling with committing to recovery. Once your client is more secure in her living situation, she may be better able to consider sobriety and to build motivation for committing to recovery.

SUD targeted case management interventions can take place at all stages of change. They respond to urgent needs in your client's life. These urgent needs can recur. It's not unusual for a client to lose housing during a relapse. It's also not unusual for a client to realize that she needs to further her education to obtain secure employment. In other words, *attending to basic needs is not adjunctive to substance use disorder treatment—it is an integral and recurring part of treatment.*

Assisting with resource gathering to meet your client's basic needs is a collaborative effort. We are working with, not just for, our clients. We help to create pathways and options, but we don't make choices for them. Case management work is hard, as resources are often scarce. It's important to show your client that you care about her basic needs and to model for her how to be persistent when pursuing resources. In the initial stages of recovery, your client may need a lot of hands-on help. She may not know who to contact for housing assistance, how to ask for food assistance, how to get to an appointment, or what to ask during one.

Additionally, many of our clients who are struggling with addiction may be court involved due to addiction-related charges and convictions. Court involvement can be experienced as an additional burden by our clients, and they may need help with:

- learning to maneuver through the court system;

- learning to make their voice be heard in a respectful manner by the court; and

- understanding court-mandated services and requirements.

While the prior section (Psychotherapy Intervention) was structured around the Stages of Change, the section outlining SUD targeted case management interventions is not. As a case manager, you should constantly assess your client's problems and needs and use these interventions as her situation requires. Basic needs such as housing, food, education, and human connections should always be addressed as quickly as possible and, if needed, repeatedly. Over time, your client will learn to meet her own needs as you are teaching her how to do so. You are not solving your client's problems; you are demonstrating for her how problems can be solved so that she can eventually do so on her own. Emphasize that asking for help is always OK no matter how far one has come in recovery. Things can feel overwhelming at any stage.

All of the following SUD targeted case management activities are for use with individuals.

If you are calling an outside agency on your client's behalf and are disclosing information about your client, you will need to complete an ROI (Release of Information) form first. If you are just receiving information, such as times for food pickup, and not disclosing client information, you do not need an ROI.

INTERVENTION 32

Safe Shelter

Many clients who struggle with addiction are at risk of becoming homeless or are functionally homeless, meaning they have a place to stay, but it is not theirs and not permanent. They often share space with others who are struggling with addiction, and this can create a precarious environment for those looking to recover from addiction. Safe and stable housing can be instrumental in creating a safe and stable recovery environment. Always ask about this, and offer assistance with developing a plan to obtain safe and stable housing. As always: Don't make promises you can't keep. We often can't put our clients into safe and stable housing immediately, but we can help them increase safety and stability step by step.

Goal: Reduce impact of substance use on client functioning and/or relationships.

Method: Client will increase living skills and independently implement skills to promote recovery.

What you will need: Paper, markers, glue, notebook to give to client. Housing resource list for your community. Internet access (phone will suffice).

1. Welcome your client and begin with empathy. Say things like this: *It can be hard when there are so many obstacles. It can feel overwhelming. But you are not alone.*

2. Introduce today's task: Identifying and addressing housing needs. You can explain: *It's so much harder to think about recovery when you don't know where you are going to sleep tonight.*

3. Work on today's task: Begin by asking your client about his living situation. Ask questions like these:

   - *Where did you sleep last night?*

   - *How about the night before?*

   - *In what way are the places you sleep safe? In what way are they unsafe?*

   - *How many people are using drugs where you are sleeping?*

   Listen carefully. Try not to interrupt, but provide validating responses, like:

   - *That sounds tough!*

   - *It sounds like you did not feel safe.*

   - *It sounds like you are tired of living with fear and uncertainty.*

4. If your client indicates, even just a little bit, that he is seeking safe and stable housing, say something like this: *Safe and stable housing is so important. It can create a pathway to a better life. Would you like to work on this together?*

5. If your client indicates that he needs a place to stay for the night, use your phone to search for the closest emergency shelter. Find out if he is willing and able to call. If he is, be there to support him and help him make plans to go to the shelter. Try not to delay. The events of the rest of the day may interfere with your client's ability and willingness to go to the emergency shelter.

You can say: *I know this is just an emergency shelter. This is a temporary thing, and we will work together to find a more long-term solution. For tonight, you can be safe in this shelter, and that matters.*

6. If the first emergency shelter is full, move on to the next one. Model persistence and self-advocacy. Don't give up.

7. Give your client the notebook you brought for him. Ask him to take notes about all shelters you have called using the following format:

Shelter name:	Shelter phone number and address:	Outcome of call:

Figure 46

You may need to draw this chart for him or print it and glue it into his notebook. If your client uses a cell phone, ask him to take a picture of the completed chart. This will be his backup in case he loses his notebook.

8. Once you have identified a shelter with an opening, help your client arrange for transportation. You may have to transport your client to the shelter.

9. Use the notebook to help your client outline the steps he needs to take to get to the shelter in a very basic way. Keep in mind: You are not just helping your client find shelter; you are teaching basic daily living skills. Keep the list of steps short, though. Your client may not be able to manage lists with more than three steps if he is still struggling with active addiction or is newly in recovery.

10. If you need to outline more than three steps, create one list with your client, work through it, then create another short list. Using the notebook, follow these steps until you are done. Make sure that your client takes notes outlining every step. Teach him to check off a step once it has been completed.

11. If your client is still struggling with active addiction or is new in recovery, you may have to be his scribe for a while. Creating a plan requires the ability to conceptualize, and your client may not be ready for this. But always be clear that it's his plan and his notebook.

12. Once your client is safely at a shelter or another safe location, schedule a follow-up appointment for the next day to make plans for longer-term housing. Many shelters offer assistance with this. Continue to use the notebook and the three-steps method until your client is able to use longer lists.

13. Remember that setbacks like getting kicked out of a shelter or relapse are part of the recovery process. Recovery is a new planet with unfamiliar rules and language, and your client needs to learn to maneuver these. Say reassuring things like this:

    - *We will try again.*

    - *Barriers are there to be overcome.*

    - *You don't have to be perfect; you just have to begin to walk into the direction of safety.*

14. If your client is not ready to move into a shelter, understand that commitment is built over time. You can present options and open doors. Continue to support him with meeting his other basic needs until he is ready to take the next step. Present options and open doors. Your positive, accepting, and supportive relationship is your most important tool. Never shame your client for making a mistake. Shame is very powerful and can increase risk of relapse and ongoing use.

15. Summarize: You have made a plan to begin working on safe and stable housing. Explain that this is a work in progress, but every day and night spent safely is a step in the right direction.

16. Assign homework: Ask your client to take notes about other needs or plans in his notebook. If he would rather draw, that is OK, too.

17. Conclude with words of encouragement like these: *You can take steps toward safe and stable housing. You don't have to do this alone. Safe and stable housing can make your life a lot better!*

INTERVENTION 33

Food

For someone struggling with active addiction, food can be an afterthought. When your client's mind is focused on feeding the addiction, it is not focused on grocery shopping (if there's even money available) and making healthy meals. Those struggling with active addiction often eat what is available: highly processed, high-sugar and high-salt foods that are inexpensive and easy to find. Helping your client recognize the need to properly feed the body and find ways to do so is a great way to teach her about her needs in general. Connecting your client with food resources is a great way to demonstrate the importance of eating well—and that you care not just about her sobriety, but her well-being.

Goal: Reduce impact of substance use on client functioning and/or relationships.

Method: Client will increase living skills and independently implement skills to promote recovery.

What you will need: Paper, markers, glue, notebook to give to client. Food resource list for your community. Internet access (phone will suffice).

1. Welcome your client and begin with empathy. Say things like this: *Things are difficult right now. It's not easy to live day to day. A lot of people may not understand what your life is like. But you are not alone.*

2. Introduce today's task: Identifying and addressing food resource needs. You can explain: *We all have to eat. Addiction has told you for a long time that it is more important than food. But your body disagrees with that assessment. You need food to live and be well.*

3. Review last week's homework: Ask your client to take out her notebook and look together at what needs or plans she has identified. Make a plan to address needs together using the three-step method. If your client has identified any plans or dreams, say something like this:

   - *This is great! You are making plans that will take you beyond addiction. Congratulations!*

   - *Just being able to think about plans for the future is a good sign.*

   - *This is exciting! You are thinking about building your life. Let's focus on that.*

   Help your client elaborate on plans or dreams in the notebook. Ask her to explore these in depth with her therapist. Explain that exploring plans can be a great way to gain motivation for sobriety and recovery.

4. Work on today's task: Ask your client:

   - *When is the last time you ate?*

   - *When you last ate, what did you eat?*

   - *How often did you skip a meal in the past week?*

   - *What is currently in your fridge and cupboards?*

Listen carefully. Make a note of any indication that your client is not getting enough nutrition and is lacking access to food. Avoid judgmental responses.

Things you should not say:	Things you should say:
I can't believe you chose drugs over food.	It's tough when you run out of money for food.
It's your own fault you ran out.	Let's find a way to get you some food while you are struggling financially. Everyone has to eat.
I don't understand why you can't just make food a priority.	When addiction takes over, it pushes every other need out of the way. That is not an easy thing to experience. Let's find a way to ensure you eat every day.

Figure 47

5. If your client indicates that she frequently goes hungry or does not eat a meal (she may not feel hungry when she is struggling with active addiction), ask if you could make a plan together to access a local food bank or other food resource.

6. Ask your client to take out her notebook. Suggest that you call a local food bank together. If your client is ready to make the call, ask her to write the number in her notebook. Draw the following chart or print it and glue it in the notebook:

Food bank/resource name:	Phone number and address:	Outcome of call:

Figure 48

Explain that it may take more than one call to obtain a food resource. Ask your client to log every call and the outcome. Model persistence. Remember: You are not just helping your client obtain food; you are also modeling how to solve problems one step at a time. Additionally, the log in your client's notebook can serve as a resource when she is in need again. When the log is completed, ask her to take a picture of it with her cell phone in case she loses her notebook.

7. If your client is in dire need, continue to make calls until you have found a source of food. Think outside the box: Look for client relatives who may be willing to help with food, even if they do not want anything else to do with her. Also look for locations that serve a hot meal. If your client is struggling with active addiction, she may not have had a real meal for quite some time.

8. Make sure you make a realistic plan. If your client needs transportation, help arrange this. If your schedule allows and it is appropriate, transport the client. Transporting shows a real understanding and willingness to take her needs seriously. Of course, you have to make sure that your client understands that you are not a bus service.

9. Once you have identified a food resource, help your client make a plan to regularly use it. This may mean scheduling regular food pickups. Remember, you are modeling how to plan ahead and take better care of oneself.

10. Summarize: You have identified a need and planned for a way to meet it.

11. Ask your client to explore her need for nurturance with her therapist. Explain that we often feel that we don't deserve to be nurtured. We minimize our need to be nurtured, be it through food or nurturing relationships. You can say something like this: *You may find that as you are beginning to feed your body, your willingness to let others nurture your soul also increases.*

12. Assign homework: Ask your client to use her notebook to jot down a few notes about her food intake for three days. Because of addiction, your client may not yet be able to discern if she is eating enough.

13. Send your client home with words of encouragement like these: *You deserve to feed your body well. You deserve to be nurtured.*

INTERVENTION 34

Good Company

Active addiction eventually becomes more important than any friendship or family relationship. But being in the company of nurturing, sober friends can be invaluable. Those are the friends who will support you when you are in need. The following intervention is designed to help your client begin to think about the importance of safe, supportive, and sober connections and create a plan for developing them.

Goal: Reduce impact of substance use on client functioning and/or relationships.

Method: Client will learn refusal skills, decrease association with other substance users, and increase association with sober supports.

What you will need: Poster board, paper, markers, glue, notebook to give to client. Support group and community activities list for your community. Internet access (phone will suffice).

1. Welcome your client and begin with empathy. Say things like:

    Addiction can make you feel all alone in spite of being surrounded by people. It's hard to feel that alone. Addiction can also make you feel lost and worthless. It's tough to feel that way. But there are people around you who see you for who you are: a worthy person who may be in pain.

2. Introduce today's task: Thinking about and beginning to plan for safe, supportive, and sober connections. You can explain it like this: *There are a lot of hurt people in addiction. Hurt people tend to hurt people. But people can recover and build each other up instead of tearing each other down.*

3. Review last week's homework. Ask your client to take out his notebook and look together at what needs or plans he has identified. Make a plan to address needs together using the three-step method. If your client has identified any hopes or dreams, say something like:

    - *This is great! You are making plans that will take you beyond addiction. Congratulations!*

    - *Just being able to plan a good meal can be a good sign.*

    - *This is exciting! You are thinking ahead to what you will eat and do next week. This is a great step forward.*

4. Work on today's task: Ask your client:

    - *How many of the people you hang out with are still struggling with active addiction?*

    - *In what ways have people around you been supportive of you as a person?*

    - *In what ways have they been supportive of you becoming sober?*

    - *What has been difficult in relationships?*

Learn as much as you can about his struggles in relationships with people who are not yet sober. Reinforce the idea that addiction can make it difficult to have supportive connections by saying things like this:

- *Addiction does have a way of coming first, even pushing aside friendships.*
- *It's hard to be around people who are still in active addiction when you are trying to be sober.*

Don't devalue your client's current friendships with people who are still struggling with active addictions, and don't shame your client for his current friends. Listen for his desire to be respected, supported, and nurtured in his relationships, then provide positive feedback for sharing that desire.

5. Using a poster board, create a visual representation of your client's connections with dots labeled with names. Your client is in the center. Those closest to him are marked close to him with a dot (and their name). Use red dots for people also struggling with addiction and blue dots for people who are sober or solidly in recovery. You should end up with an image like this:

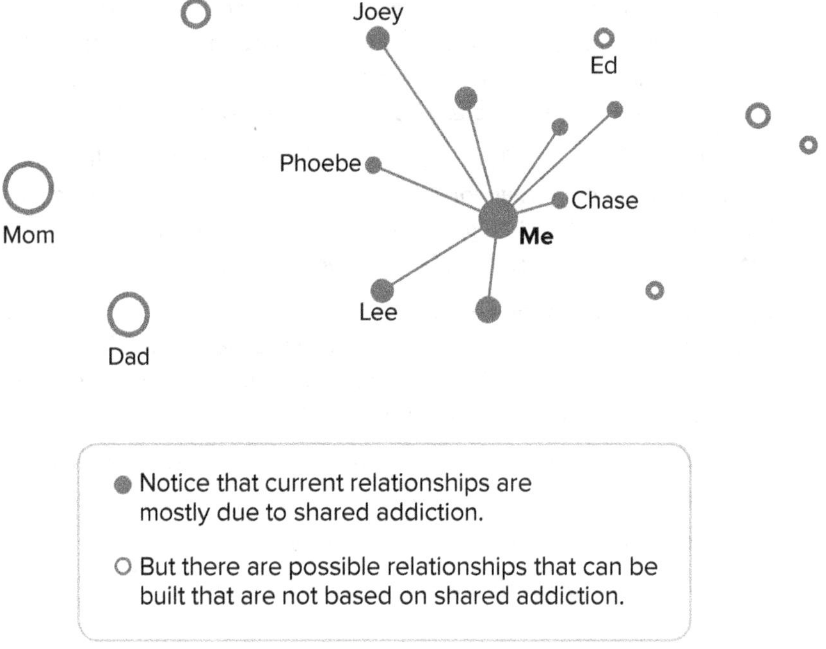

Figure 49

6. Ask your client to take out his notebook and list three friends or family members he is connected with or was when he was sober. Ask the following questions:

- *What did you feel like when you were around______________________* (insert name of person)*?*
- *What did this person say to you when you were feeling sad or lonely?*

- *What did this person do for you or with you when you were feeling sad or lonely?*

Listen with care. Simply validate all the positive experiences with friends and family your client had by saying: *You can have those kinds of connections again. You can work on creating supportive and nurturing relationships.*

7. Ask your client to circle anyone in his notebook with whom he is still connected.

8. Next, ask your client to list three sober and supportive people he would like to have closer relationships with. Explain that, at least at the moment, the focus in not on romantic relationships.

9. If your client can't think of a person from his sober past or a person who is sober right now and could become a friend, help him identify at least three local support or recreational groups. Use your phone to find when these groups meet.

10. Summarize: You have examined your client's current relationships. You have identified people with whom he might be able to build sober and supportive relationships, or groups that could help with this.

11. Assign homework: Ask your client to choose one sober and supportive person to connect with over the next week, or one sober activity to engage in with others. Ask him to give himself a checkmark when he has accomplished either.

12. Send your client home with words of encouragement like these: *You deserve to be supported. You can also be a good friend to someone else. You can build new relationships or rebuild old ones.*

INTERVENTION 35

Minding the Body

Addiction becomes all-consuming. In the end all that matters is accessing and using the drug of choice. The body itself becomes an afterthought. It may hurt, it may send a multitude of signals that it is in dire trouble, yet addiction will continue to insist that none of these signals matter. Additionally, there is often secrecy associated with addiction. When you see a medical professional, that professional may be able to recognize signs of addiction that your client is not ready to reveal. Shame also matters. Addiction is still highly stigmatized and, for this reason, your client may not be ready to disclose addiction to a medical professional. All of these factors combined can lead to a profound neglect of the body. For this reason it is important that you teach your client to once again pay attention to and take care of the body.

Goal: Reduce impact of substance use on client functioning and/or relationships.

Method: Client will increase living skills and independently implement skills to promote recovery.

What you will need: Paper and markers. Notebook to give to client. Glue. Resource list for your community.

1. Welcome your client and begin with empathy. Ask:

   - *What did you enjoy over the last few days?*

   - *Who did you connect with?*

   - *What steps did you take to take good care of yourself?*

   Highlight any actions or interactions that contributed to sobriety and recovery, no matter how small. Recognize her struggles and avoid judgmental language.

2. Introduce today's task: Learning to recognize and take care of the body's needs. You can explain the task like this: *Addiction often leads us to disregard the messages our body gives us. This can lead to neglecting our body's needs. As you work toward recovery, it is important to take care of your body.*

3. Review last week's homework: Ask your client to take out her notebook and look together at what needs or plans she has identified. Make a plan to address needs together using the three-step method. If your client has identified any hopes or dreams, say something like:

   - *I can see that you are beginning to look toward the future.*

   - *This is a wonderful step to take.*

   - *There is more to life than the burden of addiction.*

4. Work on today's task: Give your client a worksheet with the following image:

Mark all of the parts of your body that are
giving you trouble or are hurting.

Figure 50

Ask her to mark all parts of her body that are giving her trouble or hurting. Then ask her to draw a line from the troubled or hurting part to the side of the figure and label the issue—shoulder stiffness, stomach pain, etc.

5. Ask your client to describe each trouble or hurt. Listen with care and validate her concerns.

6. Ask how long it's been since she has seen a medical professional about any of these issues. If she has not seen a doctor in the past couple of months or is indicating concerning symptoms, suggest that she make an appointment.

7. Help your client select a medical provider and make a call for an appointment. If she struggles with words to use, here is a sample script:

Hi, my name is ________________________________ .

I have not seen a doctor in ________________________

    and I am experiencing the following medical issues:

____

____

____

When is your next available appointment?

Figure 51

8. Ask your client to write the appointment in her notebook and enter it into the calendar on her cell phone.

9. Give your client the body worksheet and ask her to take it to her appointment. Also ask her to take a photo of it on her cell phone as a backup.

10. If your client indicates that she does not have health insurance, assist her with applying for Medicaid or another appropriate plan.

11. Understand that some clients are pain-medication seeking. If you get the impression that your client is seeking to obtain an addictive pain medication such as an opioid painkiller, advise her that she must tell the doctor about her history of addiction. Be direct but kind. Say:

   - *Prescription medications can be addictive.*

   - *Painkillers such as Oxycodone are addictive.*

   - *You must talk with your doctor about your history of addiction.*

12. Ask open-ended questions about her willingness to maintain sobriety. With your client's explicit permission (ROI), collaborate with her psychiatrist about medication management.

13. Help your client plan for her trip to the doctor. You may have to assist with transportation on a one-time basis. Then, help her make alternative plans such as using public transportation or, if appropriate, transportation services for the disabled, or assistance from a relative or sober friend.

14. Follow up with your client about the appointment. If your client attended, ask how the appointment went. Provide positive feedback about taking care

of the body. If your client missed the appointment, ask what got in the way and help her make a better plan for the next appointment.

15. Summarize: You have helped your client recognize the need to take care of her body and have made a plan to do so.

16. Assign homework: Ask your client to identify one simple thing she can do every day to take care of her body. Give her the following homework chart to complete and bring back to your next meeting:

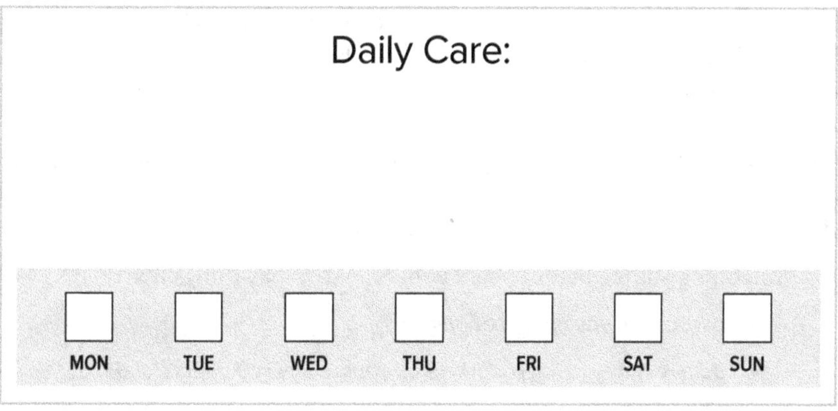

Figure 52

17. Send your client home with words of encouragement like these: *Taking care of the body is a great way to be kind to yourself. When your body begins to feel better, your mind will, too. You can take care of your body one simple step at a time.*

INTERVENTION 36

Constant Cravings

Sobriety is a commitment, but is also a process, a daily task. It's difficult to break a habit when nothing replaces the habit. Similarly, addiction demands attention through cravings. Cravings can't simply be ignored. They are a very physical experience. Your client's therapist can help him learn how to listen to, accept, and manage cravings. You, the case manager, can help him develop activities that will push the cravings into the background. This does not mean that they will be gone; rather, it means your client will be busy with other things that help him manage cravings.

Goal: Client will develop skills to manage thoughts, feelings, and situations without substance use.

Method: Client will increase living skills and independently implement skills to promote recovery.

What you will need: Index cards and markers. Rubber band.

1. Welcome your client and begin with empathy. Say things like this:

    - *I am so glad you are here again.*

    - *I admire how you keep working on your recovery. I understand that this is hard work.*

    - *I respect your hard work on your recovery.*

2. Introduce today's task: Creating a list of activities and experiences to manage cravings. You can explain the task like this: *Cravings can be strong. You need something to manage them. Engaging in another activity or experience is a good way to manage cravings.*

3. Review last week's homework: Ask your client to take out his notebook and look together at what needs or plans he has identified. Make a plan to address needs together using the three-step method. If your client has identified any hopes or dreams, say something like:

    - *Your dreams are worth pursuing.*

    - *You can make plans to begin to make your dreams come true, one step at a time.*

    - *Planning is a way to bring dreams to life.*

4. Work on today's task: Ask your client to tell you about a situation in which he experienced strong cravings. Ask how he was able to resist. If he was not able to resist the cravings, say something like this:

    Cravings are an intense experience. This is why we need to plan for them. You need a way to push the cravings into the background. One way is to do something that is important to you or that you really enjoy. Let's identify those things in order to help you resist cravings.

    Validate your client's experiences of cravings. Cravings are not just another thing that happens in your client's life. They are intense. You can compare cravings to a relentless bully. Just when you think the bully is gone, he might show up again. It's good to know the bully's route and to walk a different one.

5. Give your client ten index cards. Ask him to label those cards with activities or experiences that have the potential to help him manage cravings. Tell your client to choose activities or experiences that fully engage him such as:

    - dancing to a favorite song;

    - eating an orange;

    - taking a warm bath;

    - going for a run or walk;

    - playing with a child;

    - taking the dog for a walk; and

    - attending a sober activity with friends.

    If your client struggles with identifying activities or experiences, ask:

    - *When is the last time you laughed wholeheartedly with someone?*

    - *When is the last time you felt exhausted in a good way?*

    - *When is the last time you felt that something tasted or smelled incredibly good?*

    Use your client's answers as the basis for identifying activities to combat cravings. Generally speaking, it is easier to resist cravings in the presence of sober and supportive friends or family. When in doubt, add a sober and supportive friend to the situation.

6. Ask your client to illustrate the activities on the index cards using markers. Or he can use colors to convey the good feeling of the activity. Ask your client to only use colors that convey a good feeling to him.

7. Look at each card together and ask your client when and how he could use this card to combat cravings. If he doesn't seem certain he can, choose another card. Remember: When in doubt, add a sober and supportive person to the activity or experience.

8. Summarize: You have educated your client about cravings and made a plan for activities and experiences your client can engage in when he experiences cravings.

9. Assign homework: Give your client a rubber band to secure the activity cards. Ask him to carry the cards with him and use them as needed.

10. Closing: Send your client home with words of encouragement like these: *Cravings can be strong, but they come and go. You can make it through strong cravings with the help of these activities and experiences. When in doubt, add a sober and supportive person to any activity or experience to make it more powerful.*

INTERVENTION 37

Intimacy and Recovery

Recovery is a wonderful thing. But it is also a scary thing. It is hard to work on sobriety every day. Biologically, we are driven not to be alone. When we feel overwhelmed, we may take refuge in the company of others. Physically, others can help us feel better, at least temporarily. Sexual intimacy may make us feel alive. But sexual intimacy is also tricky, especially in recovery. Sex can become a replacement for other intense experiences such as drug use. For those new in recovery, it is important to re-examine ways of being intimate to ensure that relationships are safe, sober, and supportive. Keep in mind that many clients who are in recovery have also experienced sexual trauma. Communicate with your client's therapist about her need to process sexual and other traumatic events.

Goal: Reduce the impact of substance use on client functioning and relationships.

Method: Client will increase living skills and independently implement skills to promote recovery.

What you will need: Index cards and markers.

1. Welcome your client and begin with empathy. Say things like this:

   - *Addiction can drive you into isolation.*

   - *Being alone is difficult.*

   - *I am so glad you are here and seeking help. You are no longer alone. Recovery begins with human connection.*

2. Introduce today's task: Learning about and managing sexual intimacy in recovery. You can explain the task like this:

   When struggling with active addiction, sex often happens without intimacy. It's just something the body does. It's not really about connection. In recovery you have to find a new way of being intimate, including sexually intimate, that is not just about the mechanics of sex. You have to make sure that your sexual relationships and interactions are safe, sober, and supportive.

3. Review last week's homework. Ask your client to take out her notebook and look together at what needs or plans she has identified. Make a plan to address needs together using the three-step method. If your client has identified any hopes or dreams, say something like:

   - *I love the way you are beginning to build your future.*

   - *It's good to look forward.*

   - *There is pain in the past and about the past, but there is also hope for the future.*

   - *Dreams are the first step toward building the future you want.*

4. Work on today's task: Because sexual relationships and behavior is difficult for many to discuss, begin by saying this:

It's difficult to talk about sex. Yet, sex and sexual intimacy are an important part of adult life. Let's try to find out what supports your recovery and what may hinder it when it comes to sexual behaviors and relationships.

5. Show your client the following image:

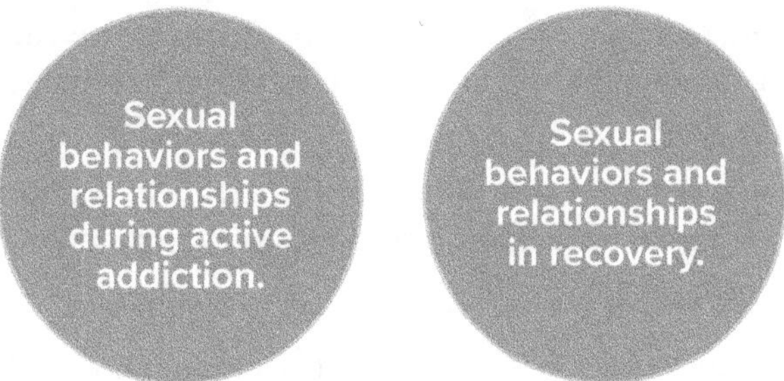

Figure 53

6. Have your client first tell you about sexual behaviors and relationships during addiction by asking the following questions:

    - *When did sexual behaviors and relationships happen in addiction?*

    - *What were the consequences of sexual behaviors and relationships during active addiction?*

    Don't assume that your client's sexual behaviors and relationships during active addiction were all harmful. Kindness can be found in all kinds of circumstances. But highlight how addiction increases risk of unsafe behaviors and harm. Make it clear that you don't judge your client for what she has done or what has been done to her.

7. Ask: *What would a safe, sober, and supportive sexual relationship look like for you?*

    Take notes on her response.

8. Ask about behaviors from the time during active addiction that may continue. Ask:

    - *In what way do these old behaviors work for you now?*

    - *In what way do they not work for you now?*

    - *What new skills or ways of managing yourself or others do you need in order to begin building safe, sober, and supportive intimate relationships?*

9. Help your client create a list of guidelines about safe, sober, and supportive intimate relationships. The guidelines should be simple. Here are some examples:

    - I will only be sexually intimate with others who are sober when I am sober.

    - I will not seek sex with someone I don't really care about just because I need something to make me feel better.

- I will take time to learn about how sexual intimacy works for me now that I am sober before I engage in a sexually intimate encounter with someone.

When writing the guidelines, use your client's words.

10. Summarize: You have discussed how sexual encounters during active addiction are different than those during sobriety. You have created guidelines for sexual intimacy that are in line with your client's values to help her with decision making.

11. Assign homework: Ask your client to write a short paragraph about what she seeks in her romantic relationships by answering the following questions:

    - How do I know I want to be intimate with someone?

    - How much time do I need to make decisions about being intimate with someone?

    - Who can I confide in to make sure that an intimate relationship I am considering will be safe, sober, and supportive?

    - Ask your client to bring the written paragraph to your next meeting.

12. Closing: Send your client home with words of encouragement like these: *It's possible to build new ways of being intimate with others that are respectful of your needs and wants. You can let your values guide your intimate relationships.*

INTERVENTION 38

The Comfort of Routines

For those struggling with active addiction, everything is driven by the focus on drugs. It's hard to establish and maintain routines. But humans thrive on routines. They give us a sense of safety and purpose. Establishing a daily routine can be difficult for those new in recovery. The following intervention is designed to help your client establish a basic daily routine.

Goal: Reduce the impact of substance use on client functioning and relationships.

Method: Client will increase living skills and independently implement skills to promote recovery.

What you will need: Paper. Pen. Fun stickers and markers. Highlighters.

1. Welcome your client and begin with empathy. Say things like:

    - *You can be proud of all the hard work you are doing in your recovery.*

    - *I understand that some days can be a struggle.*

    - *I can see your hard work paying off.*

2. Introduce today's task: Creating and following a routine to increase a sense of safety and normalcy. You can explain the task like this: *Addiction tells us that our days must be spent chasing and using drugs. When you are in recovery, a schedule or routine can anchor you in your daily sober life.*

3. Review last week's homework: Ask your client to take out his notebook and look together at what needs or plans he has identified. Make a plan to address needs together using the three-step method. If your client has identified any hopes or dreams, say something like:

    - *You are doing a great job looking for safe, sober, and supportive relationships.*

    - *These relationships can really make a difference when sobriety becomes a struggle because they can help carry you through these struggles.*

4. Work on today's task: Provide your client with the following worksheet:

My Sober Days	
Daily Routine: Time and Place	**What I will be doing:**
Early Morning:	
Morning:	
Lunch:	
Afternoon:	
Dinner:	
Early Evening:	
Late evening:	

Figure 54

Explain that all you are trying to do today is to establish a general routine, not outline specific activities or what he will eat for lunch and dinner. You are looking to identify:

- when your client gets up and has breakfast;
- what kinds of activities he will engage in during the morning;
- what time lunch will be and where;
- what kinds of activities he will engage in during the afternoon;
- what time dinner will be and where;
- what kinds of activities he will engage in during the evening; and
- what time your client will usually go to bed.

5. Explain the importance of building a structure that aligns with that of others. This often means learning to get up in the morning, as opposed to the middle of the day, and going to bed late in the evening, not early the

next morning. If your client is working, these times are fairly easy to set (but perhaps hard to follow after years of not having a schedule). You may also have to explain how much sleep is needed every day in order to function well. Addiction can change and disrupt sleep patterns. Your client may simply not know that he needs roughly eight hours of sleep per night.

6. If your client is not yet working, suggest that he create a schedule that mimics a regular workday. He should have activities scheduled for both the morning and the afternoon. Enter all treatment activities that occur daily into the schedule. Then add additional activities, such as spending time at the library or with sober friends, or even volunteering if this is appropriate for your client.

7. Explain that too much idle time can pose a danger for recovery. Boredom can lead to using substances. Of course, learning to spend some time without being engaged in a specific activity is also important. Remind your client that putting himself in the company of safe, sober, and supportive others continues to be a great way to prevent relapse.

8. Once you have completed the schedule, ask your client if he wants to decorate it. Provide stickers, markers, and highlighters. If he does not want to, just ask him to highlight the time he gets up and the time he goes to bed and reiterate the importance of establishing a basic structure for the day.

9. Ask your client to take a picture of the schedule with his cell phone in case he loses the paper schedule.

10. Summarize: Your client has learned about the need to establish a daily routine to increase his sense of safety and normalcy. He has created this routine based on his needs and circumstances.

11. Assign homework: Ask your client to take the schedule home and post it in a prominent place. Ask him to identify a safe, sober, and supportive person to serve as a schedule buddy. This person will receive a daily text message from your client about his ability to follow the schedule.

12. Explain to your client that the schedule can be adjusted based on his experiences with it, and that you'll follow up with him weekly until he has established a basic daily routine that works for him.

13. Closing: Send your client home with words of encouragement like these: *Having a schedule that fits your needs is a great step toward safety and normalcy. You deserve that, and you deserve support to establish it. Your schedule buddy can support you.*

INTERVENTION 39

Kind Words Cards

Language matters. Our clients in recovery have often been shamed and blamed over what they have done and what has been done to them. And because of societal messages about addiction, they may shame and blame themselves. It is important to help your client learn to describe her experiences of addiction and recovery using safe, supportive, and compassionate words.

Goal: Obtain skills to maintain recovery.

Method: Client will develop alternative coping skills and implement them to manage stressors and triggers to substance use.

What you will need: Index cards. Pen. Fun stickers and markers. Highlighters. Rubber band.

1. Welcome your client and begin with empathy by asking her about her week:

   - *What experiences in the past few days have encouraged you to stay on the path of recovery?*

   - *When have you felt discouraged?*

   - *What or who has helped when you felt discouraged?*

   Validate struggles, but also highlight your client's experiences of support no matter how small. Point out her willingness to recognize and accept support by saying things like this:

   - *Learning to accept help and support is a sign of strength.*

   - *When you accept help and support, you are no longer alone.*

   - *You are making changes for good that support your recovery by being willing to recognize and accept support.*

2. Introduce today's task: Learning about the importance of safe, supportive, and compassionate language toward oneself and creating a set of kind words cards. You can explain the task like this:

   The things that others say to you can shape the way you think about yourself. The things that you say to yourself can make your day better or worse. Shaming and blaming yourself is not going to be helpful for your recovery. This is why we are going to work on a set of kind cards you can use when you are struggling with negative or hurtful messages to yourself.

3. Review last week's homework: Ask your client to take out her notebook and look together at what needs or plans she has identified. Make a plan to address needs together using the three-step method. If your client has identified any hopes or dreams, say something like:

   - *You keep walking in the direction of recovery by making plans, identifying needs, and connecting with people. Nice job!*

   - *You are building a life that includes the comfort of routines and schedules. This is a great step in the right direction.*

Give your client positive and constructive feedback for all the small steps she has taken, not just major accomplishments. Recovery is built one small step at a time.

4. Work on today's task: Explain the concept of self-talk by saying: *We often praise ourselves or put ourselves down depending on what has happened. This is called self-talk. Self-talk can be constructive or destructive. Today we are going to work on constructive self-talk.*

5. Ask: *When things are not going well, what do you say to yourself?*

   Listen with compassion and help your client understand that destructive self-talk can have negative consequences. It usually makes things worse, not better.

6. Give your client ten index cards. Help her develop ten constructive messages to herself by asking questions like these:

   - *What would you say to a small child who made a mistake?*
   - *What would you have liked your friend to say to you when you struggled with a task?*
   - *What do you often wish people would say to you?*

   Explain that constructive self-talk has to be realistic and true. Here are some examples of unrealistic self-talk:

   - I am the greatest person in the world.
   - I can accomplish anything I want.
   - The things I need and want will all come to me.

   Here are some examples of realistic and constructive self-talk:

   - I deserve to be treated with kindness.
   - It's OK to make mistakes. I am human.
   - I can do this one step at a time.

7. Ask your client to write each of the constructive self-talk messages on an index card. Ask if she would like to decorate the cards. Provide fun stickers and markers.

8. Ask your client to take a picture of each card with her phone in case she loses them.

9. Summarize: Your client has learned about the impact of self-talk and has created a set of ten constructive messages to use.

10. Assign homework: Give your client a rubber band to secure the activity cards. Ask her to carry the cards with her and use them as needed.

11. Follow up with your client about the use of the cards for several weeks. Discard cards that do not work for her and help her create new cards that do. Explain that eventually constructive self-talk will become internalized, and she may not even need the cards.

12. Send your client home with words of encouragement like these: *Being kind to yourself is a habit. You can learn this habit by using the kind cards. Eventually you will just be kind to yourself.*

INTERVENTION 40

Creating a Recovery Environment

When your client makes a commitment to sobriety, his environment does not simply change into a recovery-supporting environment. A recovery-supporting environment has to be actively created by eliminating common triggers from your client's home. The following intervention requires the case manager to visit the client's home and assess the environment with the client for common triggers that may lead to substance use.

Goal: Reduce risk of relapse.

Method: Client will increase knowledge of relapse process, identification of triggers to relapse, and relapse prevention skills.

What you will need: Paper and pen. Highlighter.

1. Welcome your client and begin with empathy by asking caring questions like these:

   - *What is difficult for you right now?*

   - *What kind of supports do you have and what kind are you missing?*

   Listen with care. Validate your client's successes and his need for additional supports. Highlight any progress he has made, no matter how small. Every small step in recovery is a step in the right direction.

2. Introduce today's task: Identifying and eliminating cues for drug use in your client's home environment. You can explain the task like this:

   - *Cues are things in our environment that can trigger us to use substances. Cues can come in many forms, such as a song that reminds us of past drug use. It's important to remove any cues that you can from the home environment because there is no need to make recovery any harder than it already is. Removing cues is a great form of self-care.*

3. Review last week's homework: Ask your client to take out his notebook and look together at what needs or plans he has identified. Address needs together using the three-step method.

4. Work on today's task: Begin by thanking your client for letting you visit his home. Say something nice about the home, no matter what. You can always find one positive thing to say. Even if the home is cluttered and the odor of the cat box hangs in the air, you can still say something nice about a picture that hangs on the wall.

5. Explain that you are going to walk around the home together to check for cues that could be a trigger to substance use. You are then going to enter the cues in the chart below. Ask where he would like to start. Look for the following kinds of cues:

Things your client can SEE:				
Posters	Pictures	DVDs	Music Videos	Games

Things your client can HEAR:			
CDs			

Things your client can TOUCH:			
Paraphernalia			

Things your client can SMELL:			
Incense	Substances-Alcohol	Clothing	Ashes

Other things that are around:			
Cell Phone #s	Substances-Alcohol	Clothing	Inhalants-Related

Figure 55

It's OK to point out cues to your client and add them to the list. Ask him about cues you may not be aware of.

6. Take a look at the cues that are present. Together, decide what should be done about each. Educate your client about the following scenarios:

    - The cue can't be removed, and your client has to learn skills to manage the cue that could become a trigger. For example, your client is staying with a smoker. Your client can ask the person not to smoke in the home, but this may not be practical. Your client's best way of managing the cue may be to try to avoid it by not being present when the person is smoking. This involves effort on your client's part.

    - The cue can be removed, and your client agrees to remove it. For example, a playlist of music that glorifies drug use. Your client can erase this playlist and replace it with songs that foster recovery.

- The cue can't be removed, but your client can avoid it. An example of this would be advertising for alcohol on television. Your client can turn off the TV to avoid further exposure to the cue.

7. Create an action plan to address every cue you have identified using the following form:

Things your client can SEE:	Action plan:

Things your client can HEAR:	Action plan:

Things your client can TOUCH:	Action plan:

Things your client can SMELL:	Action plan:

Other cues:	Action plan:

Figure 56

Be specific. When you are removing a cue, you should determine exactly where it will go. Where should your client take his video games that glorify drug use? Storing them in the house is probably not a good idea because he can still get to them. Make a note of his reluctance to give up an item and help him recognize it.

Congratulate your client for completing the important step of removing cues for drug use from his home. Explain that this is always a work in progress and that he will have to be vigilant about removing or managing other cues as they pop up.

8. Summarize: Your client has identified cues for drug use in his home, and you have made a plan for each. He has made a plan to remove the cues that he can and identified ways to manage or avoid the cues he can't remove.

9. Assign homework: Ask your client to follow through with his plan of removing cues and managing those cues that cannot be removed. Plan to meet again within a week to ensure that your client is using his action plan for removing and managing cues.

10. Closing: Encourage your client to create a recovery environment at home by saying: *It's possible to create a small oasis of recovery at home. It does not have to be perfect. Every cue you remove or manage makes recovery just a bit easier.*

INTERVENTION 41

Money in Recovery

Recovery is about becoming and being well, not simply about no longer using substances. In active addiction, money has one purpose—the means to obtain substances. Money itself can be a trigger for those in recovery. Just holding a credit card or a bill can remind your client of obtaining substances. In recovery, money takes on a different role. But many clients who are new to recovery struggle with financial issues. They may have debt and court fines to pay. The following intervention is designed to help your client look at money as something that can be used to support recovery. It also teaches your client to first use money to meet basic needs, such as housing and food.

Goal: Obtain skills to maintain recovery.

Method: Client will increase communication, decision-making, and problem-solving skills.

What you will need: Paper and pen. Highlighter.

1. Welcome your client and begin with empathy by saying: *You have come so far already. Just imagine how far you can go. I understand that the road is hard. But I can see how you are changing for good.*

    Validate client feelings. Convey hope while also recognizing her struggles.

2. Introduce today's task: Learning to manage money in recovery. You can explain: *In active addiction, money serves the purpose of obtaining drugs. Now, in recovery, money serves to fulfill your basic needs, such as housing and food.*

3. Review last week's homework: Ask your client to take out her notebook and look together at what needs or plans she has identified. Address needs together using the three-step method.

4. Work on today's task: Begin by helping your client identify her current financial situation and the way she manages money. Ask:

    - *How much money do you have coming in every month or every other week? Where does this money come from?*

    - *Where does your money go?*

    If your client has no source of income, help her apply for the appropriate public benefits. If she does not yet have a bank account, explain:

    When you don't have a bank account, you end up spending money on fees for money orders or check cashing services.

    Encourage your client to set up a checking account, but don't pressure her to do so.

5. Help your client take stock of her income and expenses using this chart:

Income	Expenses

Figure 57

6. Give your client a highlighter and ask her to mark expenses that are top priorities. Explain that money should be spent first on meeting basic needs like housing and food.

7. Help your client prioritize bill payment by marking highlighted expenses with priority numbers one through three.

8. Determine on what days priority bills need to be paid and how they will be paid.

9. If your client's expenses are greater than her income, determine together which can be eliminated. If necessary, help her make appointments with a debt counselor and the legal aid society. Don't give legal advice! If your client has questions about things like bankruptcy filings, always refer to the appropriate agency.

10. Check in with your client to ensure that the process of organizing finances does not become too stressful. Instill hope that financial difficulties are temporary and can be overcome. Say things like this:

    - *Many people struggle with managing money and debt.*

    - *Managing money and debt can be learned.*

    - *People recover from addiction, and they also recover from difficult financial situations.*

11. Summarize: Your client has taken stock of her financial situation and has learned to prioritize expenses. Explain that you will continue to help her monitor and learn to manage her financial situation with the purpose of supporting her recovery.

12. Assign homework: Ask your client to write a short paragraph in her note-book about her feelings about money, her worries, but also her hopes for the future.

13. Send your client home with words of encouragement like these:

   - *As you continue on your journey of recovery, it will become easier to manage your life, including your money. Being honest with yourself about money is a great first. Your money is now serving you, not your addiction. This is progress.*

Peer Recovery Support Interventions

Peer recovery services hold a special place in the treatment of substance use disorders. The lived experience of those who have struggled with substance abuse and are now in recovery is an invaluable resource for those who are just beginning to consider sobriety or who are returning after a relapse. Your client's peer recovery worker has "walked the walk" of addiction and sobriety. She has had experiences that those who have never struggled with addiction have not had and is uniquely qualified to support those beginning their recovery journey or returning to it.

Hope also holds a special place in the treatment of substance use disorders. The belief that things can get better is central to recovery. Hope helps us take that next step, even when it seems impossible. Peer recovery workers are the walking embodiment of that hope. They literally show your client, just by being there, that recovery is possible. Of course, there are a lot of other things peer recovery workers do: They help with the identification and development of life skills and resources and help remove barriers to recovery, all while modeling hope, personal responsibility, and the development of recovery goals. Peer recovery workers are truly beacons of hope for our clients.

Thus, peer recovery services are a great place for a holistic approach to treatment. Hope is a powerful thing. Peer recovery workers are in a unique position to support the development of hope. Hence, interventions in the following section include those that address the spiritual needs of clients in recovery. We define spirituality as any belief or way of living that connects us with a power or purpose larger than ourselves and moves us in the direction of well-being and connectedness with ourselves, others, and the world.

Holistic services help our clients move toward connected and meaningful lives by introducing them to a compassionate, caring, and connected relationship.

Peer recovery workers can provide support in many areas of recovery, including substance abuse and mental illness. They are a part of an integrated approach to treatment, integrating substance use disorder treatment with mental health treatment.

INTERVENTION 42

Finding a Sponsor

Identifying a sponsor, someone who will become a companion and helper on the road to recovery, is an important task. Our clients may not know how to identify a sponsor who is compassionate, caring, and kind, but also decisively clear when it comes to pointing out roads and people that need to be avoided.

Target Goal: Obtain skills to initiate/maintain sobriety.

Method: Client will learn refusal skills, decrease associations with other substance users, and increase associations with sober peers.

What you will need: Paper and writing tools.

1. Welcome your client and check in with her. Ask what important things have happened since you last saw her. Validate her concerns and feelings.

2. Introduce today's task: Outlining the qualities of a good sponsor. You can explain the task like this:

   A good sponsor is kind and compassionate. A good sponsor listens to you and comforts you. A good sponsor will also tell you the truth even when the truth is hard to hear. A good sponsor will tell you the truth with compassion and clarity.

3. Work on today's task: Ask your client to identify the qualities she would like her sponsor to have. You can use this chart:

Sponsor needs to be:	Reason sponsor needs to be that way:

Figure 58

4. Explore what is important to your client using the chart. Gently challenge her if she is looking for support only at the expense of necessary truth-telling. You can explain:

   It is important to pick someone who will help you grow in your recovery. This means that your sponsor should be able to challenge you when you are avoiding an important subject or when you are making choices that could put your recovery in danger. Your sponsor should have your best interest at

> *heart—this means that he should be able to tell you when your judgment is impaired by addiction-based thinking.*

Listen to your client's responses and continue to help her clarify what she needs.

5. Help your client identify other expectations related to her sponsor using this chart:

My sponsor should:	Check if yes:
Have similar experiences.	
Be available on weekends.	
Attend meetings with me.	

Figure 59

Let your client add expectations that are important to her. She can then use the expectations chart for interviewing possible sponsors.

6. Ask your client how she will identify possible sponsors and choose one. Encourage her to use both charts. Help her identify at least one trustworthy, safe, and sober person who will help her make the decision. You can explain that early in recovery, addiction can still color our decisions, even when we don't think it does.

7. Role-play with your client how to ask a person to be her sponsor. Prepare her for the possibility that he might decline:

> *It's a big responsibility being a sponsor, and if someone is not quite ready, they are doing you a favor by saying no. You should have a sponsor who is there for you as you need him to be and when you need him to be, within reason, of course.*

8. Help your client plan for her next step after someone declines.

9. Once your client has chosen a sponsor, ask if she would like you to attend a meeting to outline roles and expectations. If so, you will need your client to complete an ROI for the sponsor.

10. Summarize: Your client has identified expectations for a sponsor. She has planned for the possibility that a person will not accept the role.

11. Assign homework: Send both charts home with your client. Ask her to come up with at least two people who fit the qualities and expectations she has of a sponsor.

12. Closing: Send your client home with words of encouragement like these:

> *You are taking a wonderful step in the right direction by looking for a sponsor. You are widening your circle of support. This is good for your recovery. And you are being thoughtful about this. Being thoughtful will help you make better decisions. Nice job.*

INTERVENTION 43

Recovery Prayer/Meditation 💜

Hope is central in recovery but is not a given for all of our clients. It is built in relationships with oneself, others, the world, and a higher power or purpose. This intervention is designed to help your client search for, recognize, and build on the smallest glimmer of hope. The intervention does not require a specific faith or belief system, only a willingness to gather one's thoughts about recovery and put them in the form of a prayer or meditation.

Target Goal: Obtain skills to initiate/maintain sobriety/recovery.

Method: Client will develop alternative coping skills and implement them to manage stressors and triggers to substance use.

What you will need: Paper, writing tools. Candle (can be electronic for safety).

1. Welcome your client and begin with empathy by asking questions like these:

    - *When did you feel good about yourself in the past week and why?*

    - *When were you harsh with yourself in the past week and why?*

    Listen and give your client time to explain. Highlight the ways in which your client felt good about himself, even if just a little bit. Ask him to begin to be kind to himself.

2. Introduce today's task: Creating a recovery prayer or meditation. You can explain:

    It's important for all of us to take time for ourselves. Writing a recovery prayer or meditation helps you focus on yourself, your hopes, fears, and dreams. It's not important that what you write is perfect. It can take the form of a traditional prayer or meditation, but it does not have to. It can be long or short. All that matters is that it comes from your heart and is about you.

3. Review last week's homework: Follow up with your client about the tasks you assigned during your last meeting. If you asked him to complete a worksheet, look at it together. Ask questions about his answers and highlight any steps he took toward sobriety. If he relapsed, help him focus on understanding that this a part of the process of recovery.

4. Work on today's task: Light a candle. Electronic candles are best for safety reasons. Give your client paper and a pen and ask him to write his recovery prayer or meditation. Remind him that perfection is not required. Explain that it's OK to express sadness, anger, fear, hope, faith, gratitude, and more. It's OK to ask for things or to just want to be heard.

5. Give your client time to write the prayer/meditation. While your client is writing, you should also write or doodle. This will help him be less self-conscious. Give your client as much time as he needs, at least ten minutes.

6. If your client has questions while writing, answer them in a way that helps him refocus on the task at hand. If necessary, reassure him that it's OK to

make mistakes and cross things out. If he keeps expressing that his writing is not good enough, this could be a clinical issue that you and he should bring up with his therapist. Perfectionism can be detrimental to recovery and may need to be addressed.

7. When your client is done, place the candle between the two of you and ask him to read the prayer or meditation out loud. When he is done, give positive feedback in the form of validation. Here are some examples:

    - *You expressed so much fear with so much clarity. Just saying things out loud is an act of hope.*

    - *Taking the time to express sadness and despair can be transformational. You shared your sadness and despair with me. So we both carry it now.*

8. Summarize: Your client has written a recovery prayer or meditation and has shared it with you. You have given supportive feedback.

9. Assign homework: Ask your client to take a photo of his writing with his phone in case the paper gets lost. Then send the paper home with him and ask him to share what he has written with at least one trusted, sober, and safe friend.

10. Closing: Send your client home with words of encouragement like these: *It's good to share our hopes and fears with someone. This someone can be a higher power or a friend. Shared burdens can feel less burdensome. Shared joy grows bigger.*

INTERVENTION 44

Going to a Meeting

This intervention reframes resistance to attending meetings as reluctance. This helps remove blame and shame about struggling with meeting attendance. It also normalizes the fact that going to a meeting can be frightening—perhaps like visiting another country where no one speaks your language.

Target Goal: Obtain skills to initiate/maintain sobriety/recovery.

Method: Client will increase communication, decision-making, and problem-solving skills.

What you will need: Paper, writing tools. List of preferred local meetings.

1. Welcome your client and begin with empathy by asking questions like these:

   - *How much time did you spend alone in the past few days?*

   - *When did you wish to be more supported?*

   Listen reflectively and highlight any desire on the part of your client to be more connected and supported by safe, sober, and supportive people.

2. Introduce today's task: Overcoming reluctance about going to a meeting. You can explain the task like this:

   Going to a meeting can feel scary. You may ask yourself: Who will be there? Will they judge me? What if I relapse? Will people at the meeting like me? Am I even likable? What if they notice that I relapsed and call me on it?

   These are all valid concerns. It's hard to do something so new, especially if you have spent much of your time in the world of addiction. Facing fears can be done, though, especially with support. You don't have to do this alone.

3. Review last week's homework: Follow up with your client about the tasks you assigned during your last meeting. If you asked him to complete a worksheet, look at it together. Ask questions about his answers and highlight any steps he took toward sobriety. If he relapsed, help him focus on understanding that this is part of the process of recovery.

4. Reframe resistance about going to a meeting as reluctance. Explain that people are reluctant to do things for a reason and that it is important to respect those reasons. Explain that it is also possible to work with reluctance and overcome it.

5. Work on today's task: You can use the following chart to do so:

Reason why I am reluctant to go to a meeting:	What could make me less reluctant?	Plan for overcoming reluctance:

Figure 60

Ask your client about the reasons for his reluctance to go to a meeting. Write them down, then validate them by saying things like this:

- *It's hard to _______________________________* (insert the thing that makes it difficult for your client to go to a meeting).

- *It's OK to be reluctant. This is hard.*

- *It's like learning a whole new way of being. This takes time.*

6. Help your client brainstorm ideas for decreasing reluctance. Here are some ideas you can suggest:

    - Bringing a friend.

    - Going to a meeting where you don't know anyone.

    - Taking a soothing item to hold on to during the meeting.

    - Giving yourself permission to be silent and just listen.

    - Thinking of yourself as an observer.

    - Document your client's ideas in the second column.

7. Move on to the last column. Help your client brainstorm plans for overcoming reluctance to go to a meeting, addressing each reason. Once column three is completed, compliment him for creating a plan to overcome reluctance.

8. Summarize: Your client has identified reasons for his reluctance to attend a meeting and created a plan to make it possible in spite of his reluctance.

9. Assign homework: Ask your client to take a picture of the chart you created together, just in case the piece of paper should get lost. Then send the chart home with him. Ask him to attend at least one meeting using his plan for overcoming reluctance.

10. Closing: Send your client home with kind words like these: *Overcoming reluctance is possible one step at a time. It's easier with a plan. You have already shown that you have great ideas for overcoming reluctance. Now you can put them into practice.*

INTERVENTION 45

Friendly Meetings

All recovery meetings are different. Some are lively, some are meditative. Some can be chaotic. So picking a meeting that is a good fit is important. Just because one meeting is not right for your client does not mean she won't like another meeting. This intervention is designed to help your client understand that it's important to choose the right kind of meeting for her and that this process can involve trial and error.

Target Goal: Obtain skills to initiate/maintain sobriety/recovery.

Method: Client will increase communication, decision-making, and problem-solving skills.

What you will need: Paper, writing tools. List of local meetings.

1. Welcome your client and begin with empathy by saying things like:

    - *I am so happy you came back.*

    - *It truly makes me happy that you are working on your sobriety and recovery.*

    - *I am honored to be a part of your journey.*

2. Introduce today's task: Finding a friendly meeting, one that is right for your client. You can explain the task like this:

    Every meeting is different. Some meetings provide time for quiet reflection; some are loud and chaotic. Some meetings can be very welcoming, while others can be confusing for first-timers. This is why it is important to pick a meeting that fits who you are. The first meeting you try may not be right for you. This is OK. You just have to keep looking.

3. Review last week's homework: Follow up with your client about the tasks you assigned during your last meeting. If you asked her to complete a worksheet, look at it together. Ask questions about her answers and highlight any steps she took toward sobriety. If she relapsed, help her focus on understanding that this is part of the process of recovery.

4. Work on today's task: Help your client create a list of things she is looking for in a meeting. You can use this chart:

What I am looking for in a meeting:	Why I am looking for this:	Is expectation realistic?

Figure 61

Begin by asking your client what she is looking for in a meeting. Another way to ask would be to help her verbalize what kinds of gatherings she likes and why. This is important because sometimes we like things that do not necessarily move us forward in recovery. Here is an example: Heather does not like it when people disagree with her. She is looking for people who always agree with her. This is not a realistic expectation. Disagreements can be healthy when expressed in a respectful and helpful manner.

5. Together review your client's top three preferences. Then use your local meeting directory and the collective wisdom of the recovery community to help your client find a meeting she may want to try. It's OK to steer her away from meetings that might be unhelpful.

6. Write down the meeting details for your client and ask her to take a picture of the note with her phone. Also ask her to put the meeting in her paper or digital calendar. Ask if she needs help getting to the meeting. It's not uncommon for clients to need support to go to their first meeting. If necessary, accompany your client to the first meeting or help her identify a person who will.

7. Prepare your client for all kinds of experiences by saying things like this: *You may really like this meeting. But if you don't, that is OK. You can try another meeting if this one is not right for you.*

8. Summarize: Your client has learned about the importance of choosing a meeting that is right for her and has made a plan to attend one. She has also learned that it is OK to try another meeting if this one is not right for her.

9. Assign homework: Ask your client to attend the meeting she has chosen at the frequency that is right for her. If your client needs a lot of support, you should give her several meetings to choose from.

10. Closing: Send your client home with words of encouragement like these: *Over time, going to a meeting becomes more comfortable. It can become a source of support and strength. You just have to take the first few steps.*

INTERVENTION 46

Circle of Recovery

The following intervention is designed to show your client that recovery does not happen in isolation, that it is important to be connected to all kinds of supports in order to begin and maintain sobriety and recovery.

Target Goal: Obtain skills to initiate/maintain sobriety/recovery.

Method: Client will increase communication, decision-making, and problem-solving skills.

What you will need: Paper, writing tools. Local resource directory.

1. Welcome your client and begin with empathy by saying things like this:

   - *It's so nice to see you again.*

   - *You have been coming here for _______________________* (insert actual time span). *This means that you have remained committed to working on sobriety and recovery. Nice job!*

   - *You clearly are a strong person for coming back to work on your sobriety and recovery. It's not easy. You deserve applause.*

2. Introduce today's task: Building networks of support for initiating and maintaining sobriety and recovery. You can explain the task like this:

   Addiction often tells us that we do not need other people, that we can do all of this alone. But this is really not true. In order to be truly well, we need connections with safe, supportive, and sober people. As humans we are designed to be connected with others. We also need to be a part of larger networks of people, such as clubs, support groups, and even places of employment and faith or spiritual communities.

3. Review last week's homework: Follow up with your client about the tasks you assigned during your last meeting. If you asked him to complete a worksheet, look at it together. Ask questions about his answers and highlight any steps he took toward sobriety. If he relapsed, help him focus on understanding that this is part of the process of recovery.

4. Work on today's task: Show your client the following image:

Figure 62

Ask your client to identify as many elements as possible in his own life that correspond with this recovery map. Write the names of your client's sponsor and his friends (indicate sober, safe, and supportive friends by underlining them). Keep going until you have made a note of all the elements of the recovery map your client can name.

5. Help your client identify gaps in the recovery map. You can say:

   - *I see that you are not yet connected with a peer support worker. How can we address this?*

   - *You said you are spending a lot of time in online meetings but are not attending any live meetings. What can you tell me about this?*

   Help your client find words for reluctance to connect with people, places, or services.

6. Find out which gap your client is most willing to fill and help him create a plan for filling it. Perhaps your client does not yet have a therapist. Help him set up his first session. Explain what to expect and offer to accompany him to the building. Congratulate him on taking steps to fill his recovery map.

7. Explain that recovery works best when all kinds of supports and structures are in place. Work can often be a struggle for those newly in recovery. Normalize this experience. Then find out ways in which your client would like to contribute to the world aside from working. Helping out at a local animal shelter, even for just an hour per week, can be a great start.

8. Summarize: Your client has identified elements of his recovery map, including gaps that may need to be filled. He has created a plan for filling one gap with your help.

9. Assign homework: Ask your client to take a picture of his personalized recovery map for future reference. Then send the map home with him and ask him to connect with at least one safe, supportive, and sober person in the next few days and spend meaningful time together.

10. Send your client home with words of encouragement like these: *We all need to be connected. You are building new connections to support your recovery. Nice work. And you are connecting with those who already support you. This is so good for you.*

INTERVENTION 47

The Next Hour

In recovery some days are harder than others. On those very difficult days when life's challenges are overwhelming and cravings lurk closely, it is important to have a plan, a very specific plan. The following intervention will help your client create a short-term plan for staying sober, one that can be repeated hour by hour, if necessary, to make it through the day.

Target Goal: Obtain skills to initiate/maintain sobriety/recovery.

Method: Client will develop alternative coping skills and implement them to manage stressors and triggers to substance use.

What you will need: Paper, writing tools. Index cards. Markers.

1. Welcome your client and begin with empathy by saying things like this:

     - *I understand that sobriety is hard work.*

     - *Some days are harder than others.*

     - *I am here to support you.*

     - *Even when sobriety seems impossible, it is still possible.*

2. Introduce today's task: Finding ways to stay sober. You can explain it like this:

     There are those very hard days when you can't think about making it through the whole day sober. Sometimes it's best to just think about staying sober one hour at a time. An hour seems like a manageable amount of time. And, if necessary, you can repeat that one hour, over and over, until you have made it through the day. Let's find a way to fill that hour with people and things that keep you sober.

3. Review last week's homework: Follow up with your client about the tasks you assigned during your last meeting. If you asked her to complete a worksheet, look at it together. Ask questions about her answers and highlight any steps she took toward sobriety. If she relapsed, help her focus on understanding that this is part of the process of recovery.

4. Work on today's task: Begin by asking your client about people, places, activities, and things that are most likely to keep her connected to sobriety. Make a simple list. You can use this form:

Person most likely to help me stay sober:	1.
	2.
	3.
Place most likely to contribute to my sobriety:	
Activity most likely to contribute to my sobriety:	
Thing most likely to contribute to my sobriety:	
Other things:	

Figure 63

5. Encourage your client to pick a person who is safe, supportive, sober, and **available.** The last element is important. Who is close by, easy to reach, and willing to come over or talk on the phone? Identify a minimum of three people to ensure that at least one will be available when needed.

6. Encourage your client to pick a place that is close by and, of course, not a gathering place for current users. Explain that it is best to combine the supportive person with the safe place.

7. Ask your client to choose an activity that can easily be completed without props. It is unlikely she will have the energy to gather props when struggling with cravings. The activity should be simple and engaging. Explain that it may be best to engage in the activity with the safe person in the chosen place.

8. Ask your client to choose an item that is easily accessible and portable so she can take it with her wherever she goes. Some people carry photos of loved ones; others carry herbal tea bags. Encourage your client to show the item to her safe person and reflect on the contribution this item is making to sobriety.

9. Ask your client if there is anything else she can think of that contributes to her sobriety. If there is, put it in the "other things" category.

10. Take out an index card formatted like this:

My Sober Hour:

1. Call ____ . Talk with
____ for 15 minutes and/
or make plans to meet up at my designated sober place.

2. Engage in sobriety-embracing activity with my
designated person for at least 30 minutes.

3. Show my sobriety-enhancing item _______________ to my
designated person. Explain how it enhances my sobriety.

4. Repeat this hourly as needed. If my safe, sober, and
supportive friend cannot stay with me for the second hour,
plan together who will be there with me. Remember: It's
harder to use when a safe and sober person is next to me.

Figure 64

11. Ask your client to fill in the name of her safe, supportive, and sober person, and the sobriety-enhancing item. Then ask your client to tell you about her sobriety hour in detail. Ask open-ended questions to bring out all details.

12. Help your client look for possible gaps in the plan by asking:

    - *What could go wrong?*

    - *Is there a place you could pass on the way that could trigger you to use?*

    - *When you pick up the phone to call your sober friend, how will you make sure that you don't call your dealer?*

    Address gaps in detail. Make a plan that is as foolproof as possible.

13. Summarize: Your client has made a list of people, places, activities, and things that support sobriety. She has used this list to create a plan.

14. Assign homework: Ask your client to take a picture of her sober day plan with her phone just in case the paper version gets lost. Send the paper version home with her. Ask her to schedule a "dry run" of the plan. Of course, if there is a need to put the plan into action at any point, she should do so.

15. Closing: Send your client home with words of encouragement like these: *It's good to have a plan. You made a great plan to begin with. Use it, then make it even better. This plan can grow as you grow in your recovery.*

INTERVENTION 48

Recovery Team

When addiction takes over, family ties often break or become frayed. Addiction demands so much time and attention that there may be little left for sober family and friends. But while addiction can be pursued alone, sobriety and recovery can't. Support and connection make sobriety and recovery possible. The following intervention is designed to help your client recognize and build his recovery team.

Target Goal: Obtain skills to initiate/maintain sobriety/recovery.

Method: Client will increase communication, decision-making, and problem-solving skills.

What you will need: Paper, writing tools. Markers.

1. Welcome your client and begin with empathy by asking:

   - *What was the highlight of your last week?*

   - *When did you feel a moment of peace, no matter how brief?*

   - *What was this moment like? Did you share it with anyone?*

   Listen reflectively. Highlight even fleeting moments of mindfulness and joy. Tell your client that joy can grow rapidly, especially if shared with others.

2. Introduce today's task: Recognizing the importance of building and using a recovery team. You can explain the task like this:

   There are so many things happening when we start the journey of recovery. Lots of times we are going to need support. Sometimes we need someone to be kind. Sometimes we need a friend. Sometimes we need someone who confronts us. Sometimes we need a soft place to fall. This is why it is important to put together a team that supports recovery. When you have a team, you have backup. And when you are in recovery, it's a good idea to have as much backup as possible.

3. Review last week's homework: Follow up with your client about the tasks you assigned during your last meeting. If you asked him to complete a worksheet, look at it together. Ask questions about his answers and highlight any steps he took toward sobriety. If he relapsed, help him focus on understanding that this is part of the process of recovery.

4. Work on today's task: Ask your client about family and friends who support his recovery. Explain that any kind of support can qualify someone to be on the support team. It does not have to be extensive. Begin building a map of your client's recovery team by adding people to this image:

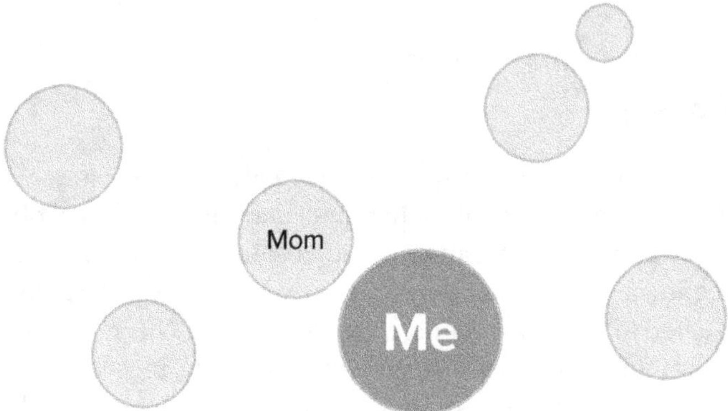

Figure 65

Label each circle with the name of a family member, friend, support professional, or acquaintance. Those most likely to support recovery substantially should occupy the closest circles. Those who provide some support, but perhaps not every day, can be farther out. Write everyone's phone numbers under their names.

5. Help your client identify family members who may be willing to support him. Though your client may be estranged from family due to addiction, it is possible that parents or siblings are willing to provide support that can grow over time. Ask him to mark all family members on the recovery team with a green circle.

6. Review the recovery team map together. Who is missing? Continue to help your client search for long-lost supports by asking questions like these:

    - *Who sends you a birthday card?*

    - *Who used to come to your house before you started using substances?*

    - *Who shut you out because they did not want you around their children due to your struggles with addiction?*

    Put those people on the fringes of the recovery team map. Over time, they may become more willing to provide support again.

7. Summarize: Your client has filled out a recovery team map including all kinds of people who support him and may support him in the future. You have paid special attention to family members who might be willing to support him now that he has made a commitment to sobriety.

8. Assign homework: Ask your client to take a picture of the recovery team map. Then send the map home with your client and ask him to hang it in a prominent spot (such as on the fridge). Ask him to call one person every day to explore what kind of support they are willing to provide, then make a note of it next to the person's name. Ask your client to bring the recovery map back to your next meeting, as it is a work in progress.

9. Closing: Send your client home with words of encouragement like these: *We all need someone to lean on. It's OK to ask for support. You deserve to be supported.*

INTERVENTION 49

Follow Your Healthy Passions

Addiction has a way of clouding judgment. We often say that we should follow our passions. But what if your passion is to play video games featuring drugs and violence all day? That's not a recovery-enhancing passion. The following intervention is designed to help your client identify a passion that enhances recovery. As a general rule: Any activity that keeps your client isolated will need modification because recovery requires human connection and support.

Target Goal: Obtain skills to initiate/maintain sobriety/recovery.

Method: Client will increase communication, decision-making, and problem-solving skills.

What you will need: Paper, writing tools. Markers.

1. Welcome your client and begin with empathy by saying: *I have gotten to know and appreciate you for who you are. I can see how hard you are working. I admire your hard work on your recovery.*

2. Introduce today's task: Identifying your client's passion and finding recovery-enhancing ways to follow it. You can explain the task like this:

    There are things we are passionate about that are not good for us. For example, playing violent video games all day, sleeping during the day, eating high-sugar, high-salt, high-fat foods, to name only a few. None of these things are bad in moderation. They only become tricky when we do too much of them. In recovery, we may have to modify some of the things we are passionate about to make them more recovery-enhancing. That is what today is about: looking at what you love to do and finding ways you can do those things in a recovery-enhancing way.

3. Review last week's homework: Follow up with your client about the tasks you assigned during your last meeting. If you asked her to complete a worksheet, look at it together. Ask questions about her answers and highlight any steps she took toward sobriety. If she relapsed, help her focus on understanding that this is part of the process of recovery.

4. Work on today's task: Find out what activities or things your client is passionate about by asking questions like these:

    -   *If you could go home right now and do anything, what would it be?*

    -   *What makes you smile and talk about it with excitement?*

    -   *What would you do if you had four weeks off?*

    Listen reflectively. Validate your client's needs without validating unhealthy expressions of those needs. Here is an example you can tell your client:

    Eric loves playing video games. He plays them as much as he can because they make him forget about his addiction to painkillers. He has missed several meetings with his sponsor because he loves his games so much.

He gets so absorbed in his games that he forgets to eat, and he no longer answers the phone for his sponsor or friends.

5. Ask your client what she thinks is wrong with the situation. Then help her identify ways in which Eric could follow his passion in a healthy way.

6. Ask your client what she is passionate about and write her answer in the left box in the image below.

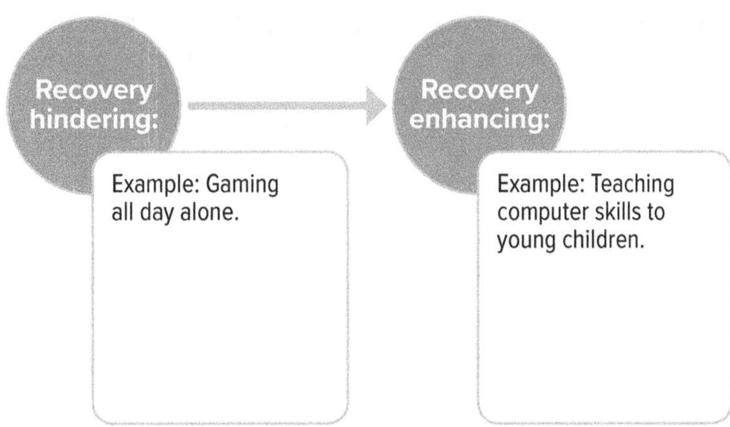

Figure 66

You can explain that, as a general rule, any activity that is completed in isolation is not recovery-enhancing, and that activities that are completed with safe, supportive, and sober friends are often recovery-promoting.

7. Ask your client to identify a way in which the activity she is passionate about could become recovery-enhancing. You can offer the following example:

Erica loves to cook and eat. Cooking keeps her mind off her cravings, and eating is just so satisfying. Erica stays home and cooks, then eats much of what she has cooked because it is there. Her friend Sonya tells her about a healthy cooking class at the local community center. Erica attends this class and meets new people. Six months later she becomes a part-time instructor for the class. Her attendance and teaching of the class are recovery-enhancing activities.

Help your client find a way in which she can make what she loves recovery-enhancing.

8. Some activities, such as video games involving drugs and violence, may need to be substantially altered in order to become recovery-enhancing. It's quite possible your client needs to give up games glorifying drug use and violence. If your client loves hanging out in bars, she will have to find other places for social interactions.

9. Summarize: Your client has learned about recovery-enhancing ways in which she can do what she loves. She has learned that most, but not all,

activities become recovery-enhancing when they happen in the company of safe, supportive, and sober friends.

10. Assign homework: Ask your client to share at least one meal per day with a safe, sober, and supportive person to make the activity of eating more recovery-enhancing.

11. Closing: Send your client home with words of encouragement like these: *Simple daily activities can become recovery-enhancing. You don't have to spend money to engage in recovery-enhancing activities. Simply adding a safe, sober, and supportive person to an activity can make many, but not all, activities recovery-enhancing.*

INTERVENTION 50

All Around Recovery

Many who are struggling with addiction are also struggling with other mental health issues, such as anxiety, depression, and posttraumatic stress disorder. Addiction and mental illness are often intertwined. They should be treated together, not separately. The following intervention will educate your client about the need to address addiction and mental illness together. Keep in mind that debating which came first, the addiction or the mental illness, is mostly useless. When we see addiction and mental illness together, both need to be addressed now because they both impact your client now.

Target Goal: Obtain skills to initiate/maintain sobriety/recovery.

Method: Client and family will be provided education regarding the client's mental health and SUD symptoms, their effect on family and school performance, and will be helped to reframe emotional and behavioral processes to engage the family around the client's behavior.

What you will need: Paper, writing tools. Local resource directory.

1. Welcome your client and begin with empathy by asking:

   - *What or who keeps you going?*

   - *When do you experience overwhelming feelings?*

   - *What kind of support do you need to manage those feelings?*

   Listen reflectively. Highlight your client's ability to express feelings. If your client expresses that he needs more support, brainstorm about putting new resources in place. Help him connect with new resources and thank him for sharing with you.

2. Introduce today's task: Learning about taking care of the whole self by addressing addiction and mental illness together. You can explain the task like this:

   Many who struggle with addiction are also walking around with the invisible burdens of depression, anxiety, trauma-related and other mental illnesses. It becomes difficult to recover from addiction when those invisible problems are not addressed. This is why it is so important also to receive treatment for a mental illness that may burden you. Recovery is all about becoming well as a whole person. This means getting treatment for all that burdens you, not just your addiction.

3. Review last week's homework: Follow up with your client about the tasks you assigned during your last meeting. If you asked him to complete a worksheet, look at it together. Ask questions about his answers and highlight any steps he took toward sobriety. If he relapsed, help him focus on understanding that this is part of the process of recovery.

4. Work on today's task: Show your client the following image:

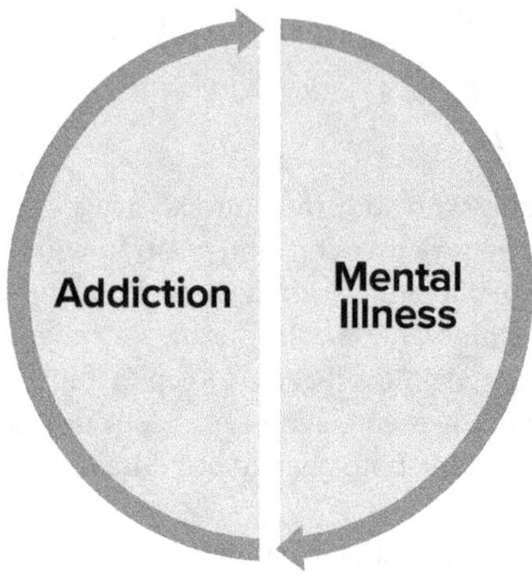

Figure 67

Ask your client the following questions to help him understand how addiction and mental illness can relate:

- *In what way do you think feeling depressed or anxious or having experienced trauma could make you more likely to look to drugs and alcohol for relief?*

- *Have you ever looked to drugs and alcohol for relief from intense feelings?*

- *In what way could struggling with addiction make you more likely to have a traumatic experience or feel anxious or depressed?*

- *Has this ever happened to you? If so, how?*

Listen with compassion. Help your client highlight the relationship between addiction and mental illness. If your client does not believe that there is a possible connection between the two, this is OK. If necessary, you can bring up the relationship between addiction and mental illness at another time.

5. If your client expresses that he is also struggling with the invisible burden of mental illness, encourage him to seek treatment for the mental illness. Explain that this will support his recovery. If necessary, help him arrange for a mental health assessment and appropriate services. If your client struggles specifically with addiction and trauma, look for a Seeking Safety group for him. The Seeking Safety curriculum is based on the book Seeking Safety (Najavits, 2003) and addresses addiction and trauma together in a way that works for many clients. The curriculum first and foremost helps clients build safety. Exposure to traumatic memories is not a part of treatment in Seeking Safety groups, because clients may not yet have the tools to manage those memories without use of drugs or alcohol.

6. Summarize: You have educated your client about the ways in which addiction and the invisible burden of mental illness can relate. You have helped your client identify additional treatment needs and have arranged to meet those needs as appropriate.

7. Assign homework: Give your client the following image to take home, complete, and bring to your next meeting.

Things I need to do to address my

____

(insert name of mental health condition)

1. _______________________________________

2. _______________________________________

3. _______________________________________

4. _______________________________________

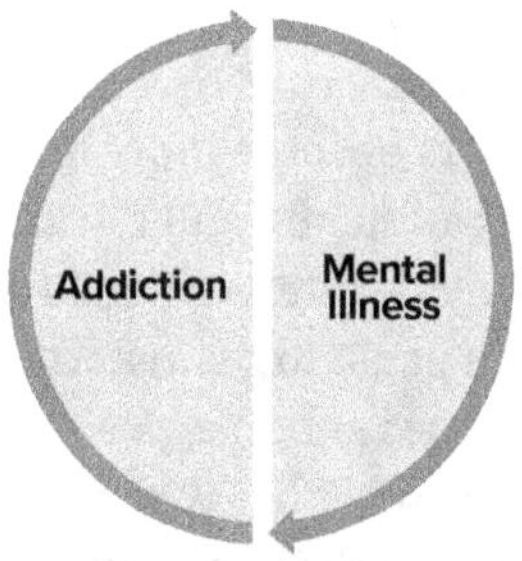

Addiction | Mental Illness

Figure 68

Ask your client to think about at least three things he could do to support his recovery from addiction and mental illness together.

8. Closing: Send your client home with words of encouragement like these: *You deserve to recover as a whole person. Taking care of all your needs can help your recovery from addiction.*

INTERVENTION 51

Hanging Out

For teenagers, peers are essential. As we grow up, we gradually move away, step by step from our parents and toward our peers to meet our relational needs. While this is frequently a source of tension between parents and teens, increased independence and connectedness with peers moves us toward adulthood. Ideally, teenagers remain meaningfully connected with their parents, reworking the relationship to match the new phase of life, while building meaningful relationships with peers.

When addiction comes into play during the teen years, relationships with peers can either enhance sobriety and recovery or support addiction. Therefore, teenagers who are on the road to recovery face an additional relational challenge: At a time when peers become more important, they need to move away from a peer group that supports addiction and toward a peer group that enhances sobriety and recovery. The following intervention is designed to help your teenage client recognize this need and begin to brainstorm about a sober peer group.

This intervention is designed for teens but can be adapted for use with adults who struggle to sever ties with peer groups that are immersed in addiction.

Target Goal: Obtain skills to initiate/maintain sobriety/recovery.

Method: Client will learn refusal skills, decrease associations with other substance users, and increase associations with sober support.

What you will need: Paper, writing tools. Local resource directory.

1. Welcome your client and begin with empathy by asking:

    - *What's been happening in your life?*

    - *Who is your main person right now, the one you call when you need support?*

    - *Who can you do without right now? Who annoys you?*

    Listen empathically and without judgment. Validate your client's need to have close friends, the kind you can call in the middle of the night when you have done something regrettable. Find out what annoys your client. Teenagers are frequently annoyed when adults give unsolicited advice and seem judgmental.

2. Introduce today's task: Looking for safe, sober, and supportive peers. You can explain the task like this:

    Addiction tells us that it's OK to hang out with people who are using drugs. That it's no big deal. That it's OK to use just this one time. When we struggle with addiction, we tend to believe these messages. As we move into recovery, we begin to realize that we can't really hang around people who are actively struggling with addiction. But what does this mean for our friendships? Who should we hang out with?

3. Review last week's homework: Follow up with your client about the tasks you assigned during your last meeting. If you asked her to complete a worksheet, look at it together. Ask questions about her answers and highlight any

steps she took toward sobriety. If she relapsed, help her focus on under-standing that this is part of the process of recovery.

4. Work on today's task: Ask your client questions to help her think about the kinds of peers she is hanging out with. Here are some questions to ask:

   - *How many of your friends are still using, even if just a little bit?*

   - *Who in that group are you worried about and why?*

   - *What would happen if you told the group you could only hang out with them if there were no drug or alcohol use?*

   Listen without judgment. Highlight the difficulties that can occur when a person new to sobriety hangs out with people who are still struggling with addiction. Use questions to highlight these difficulties. Here are some questions to ask:

   - *What is it like to be around* _________________________ (insert name of person in peer group who is not sober) *when he/she is intoxicated?*

   - *In what ways does being around peers who are using make sobriety harder?*

   - *When you observe your friend using, what do you want to do and say, and why? How do you think the group would respond?*

   - *What are your hopes for members of this group?*

5. Introduce the idea that it is important to have a group of safe, sober, and supportive peers to hang out with. Help your client brainstorm about finding a safe, sober, and supportive peer group by asking:

   - *What groups and after-school activities does your school offer?*

   - *What groups and after-school activities are offered in your community?*

   - *What groups and activities specifically for teens are offered by recovery organizations?*

6. Create a list of groups and activities your client can participate in, includ-ing those specifically for teens in recovery and those that aren't but don't include drug or alcohol use.

7. If your client expresses worry about abandoning his friends, explain that you are not asking him to. He may simply need to take a break from people who don't support his recovery. You can also encourage him to find meaningful ways to relate to those who are still actively using by inviting them to sober events and recovery-related meetings by saying something like: *"I am grateful for your friendship. I am working hard to be sober. I can't go anywhere that doesn't support my sobriety. But I would love for you to come to* [insert name of commu-nity or school event] *with me. Heads up: You can't use drugs or alcohol at this event."*

8. Summarize: You have discussed the increased importance of safe, sober, and supportive friends when in recovery. You have identified groups and activities that can provide a source of such friends. You have also introduced

a way of including current friends in safe, sober, and supportive activities or groups.

9. Assign homework: Ask your client to pick one safe, sober, and supportive activity or group and attend it. He should make contact with at least one person in the group and have a conversation. Ask him to report back on this the next time you meet.

10. Closing: Send your client home with words of encouragement like these: *You have already built important friendships. You now have a chance to build safe, sober, and supportive friendships. Congratulations on taking this major step forward.*

References

Beck, J. S. (2011). *Cognitive behavior therapy: Basics and beyond.* New York: Guilford Press.

Boehme, R. (2018). *Treating anxiety: Using cognitive behavioral therapy skills and interventions.* Berea, OH: The Institute for Family and Community Impact.

Miller, W. R., & Rollnick, S. (2013). *Motivational interviewing: Helping people change.* New York: Guilford Press.

Najavits, L. M. (2003). *Seeking safety: A treatment manual for PTSD and substance abuse.* New York : Guilford Press.

Prochaska, J. O., & Norcross, J. C. (2001). Stages of change. *Psychotherapy: Theory, research, practice, training, 38* (4), 443-448. doi:10.1037/0033-3204.38.4.443

Prochaska, J. O., Redding, C. A., & Evers, K. E. (2008). The transtheoretical model and stages of change. In *Health behavior and health education* (pp. 97-121). San Francisco, CA: Jossey-Bass.

Skinner, W., Cooper, C., Chamberlain, C., Ravitz, P., & Maunder, R. (2013). *Motivational interviewing for concurrent disorders.* New York: W. W. Norton.

Tolin, D. F. (2016). *Doing CBT: A comprehensive guide to working with behaviors, thoughts, and emotions.* New York: Guilford Press.

Appendix: Selected Figures

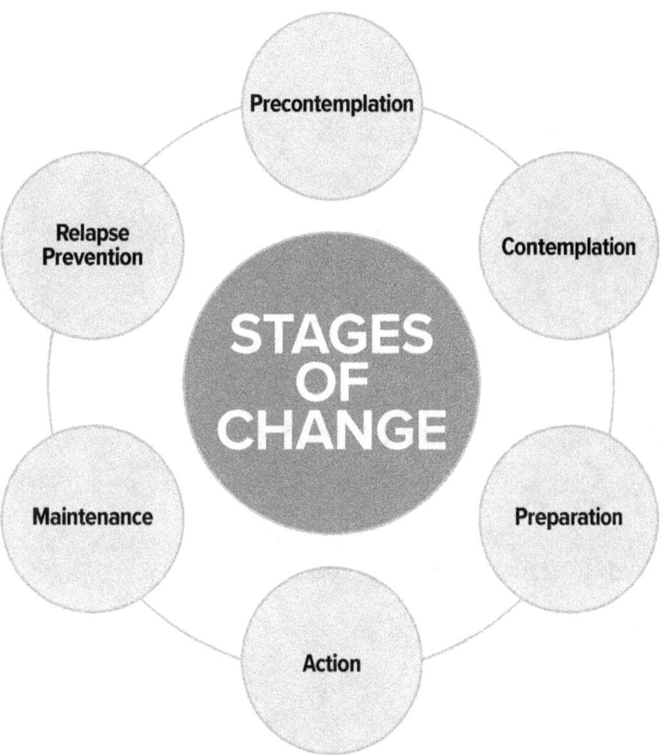

Figure 1

From *School-Based Mental Health Interventions*. © OhioGuidestone. Owners of this book are granted permission to reproduce pages for use with their clients.

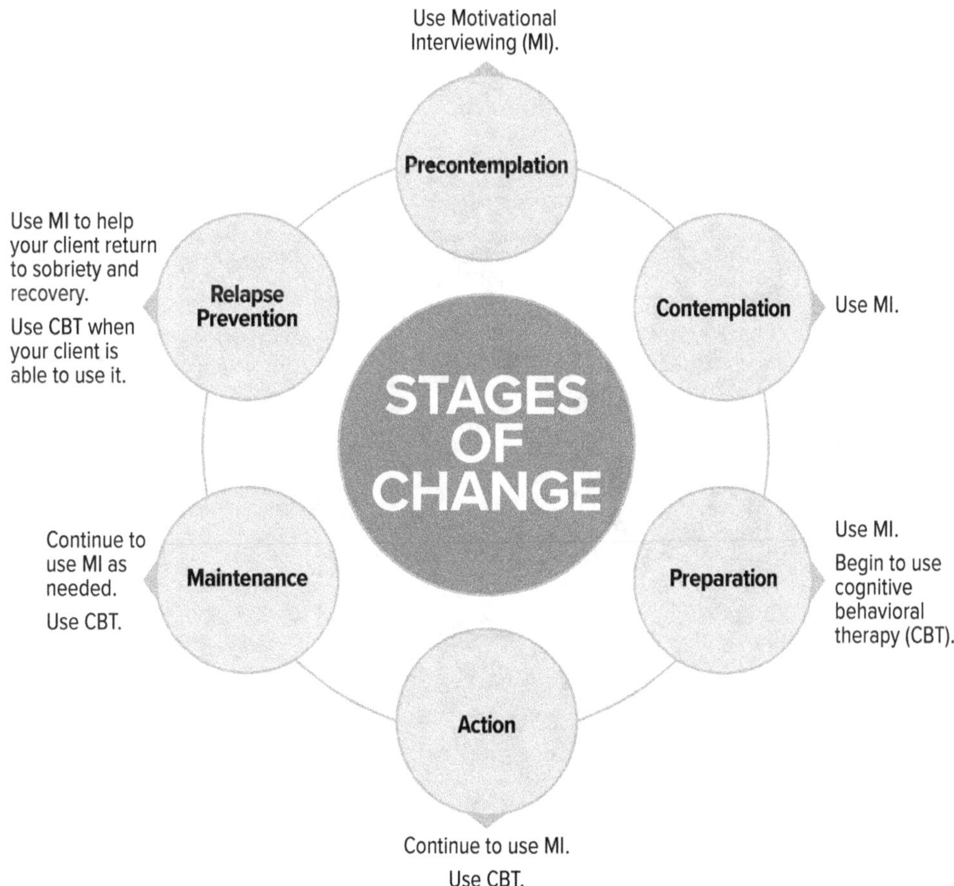

Figure 2

From *School-Based Mental Health Interventions*. © OhioGuidestone. Owners of this book are granted permission to reproduce pages for use with their clients.

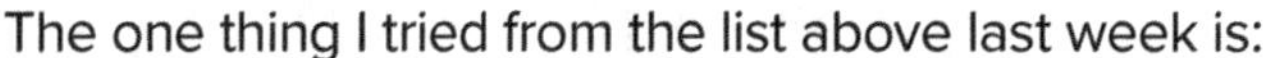

Figure 3

Figure 4

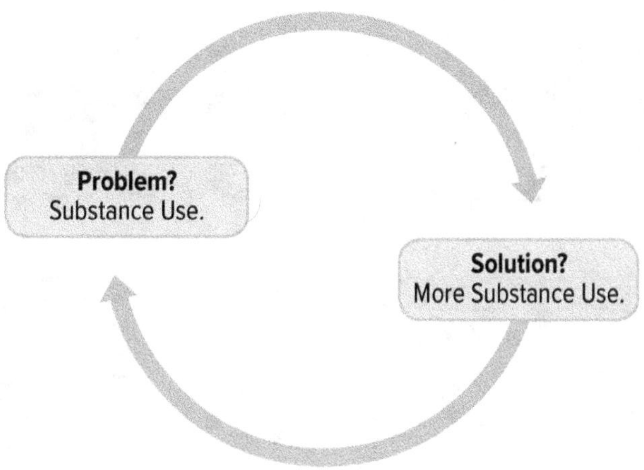

Figure 5

Things I have tried to limit my substance use or quit that did not work:	
1	5
2	6
3	7
4	8
Underline any solutions that involved more substance use or led to more substance use.	

Figure 6

Figure 7

Steps I can take to leave the prison of addiction:

1. ____

2. ____

3. ____

Figure 8

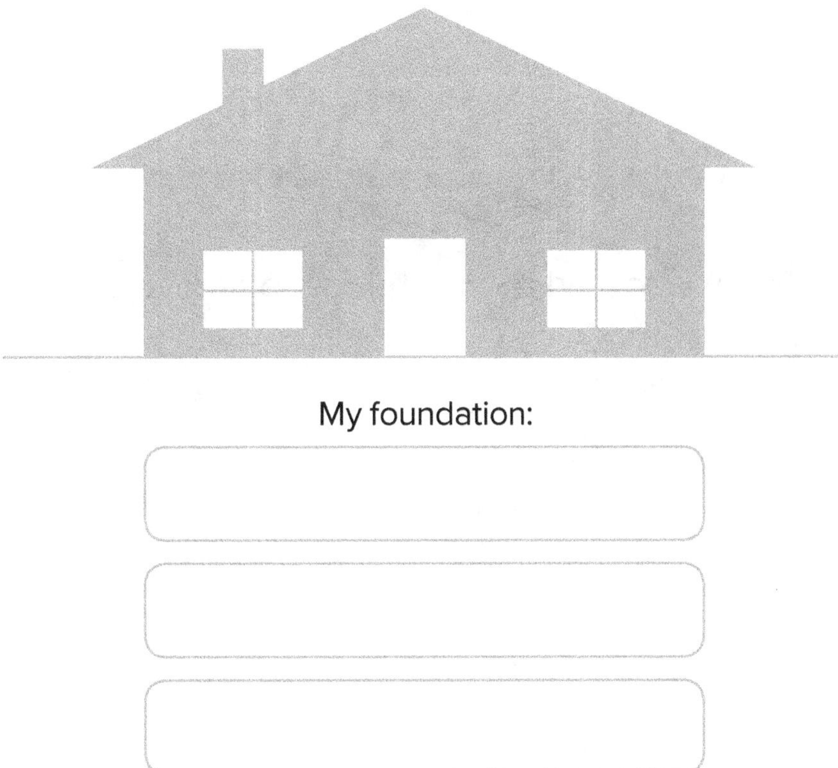

Figure 9

From *School-Based Mental Health Interventions.* © OhioGuidestone. Owners of this book are granted permission to reproduce pages for use with their clients.

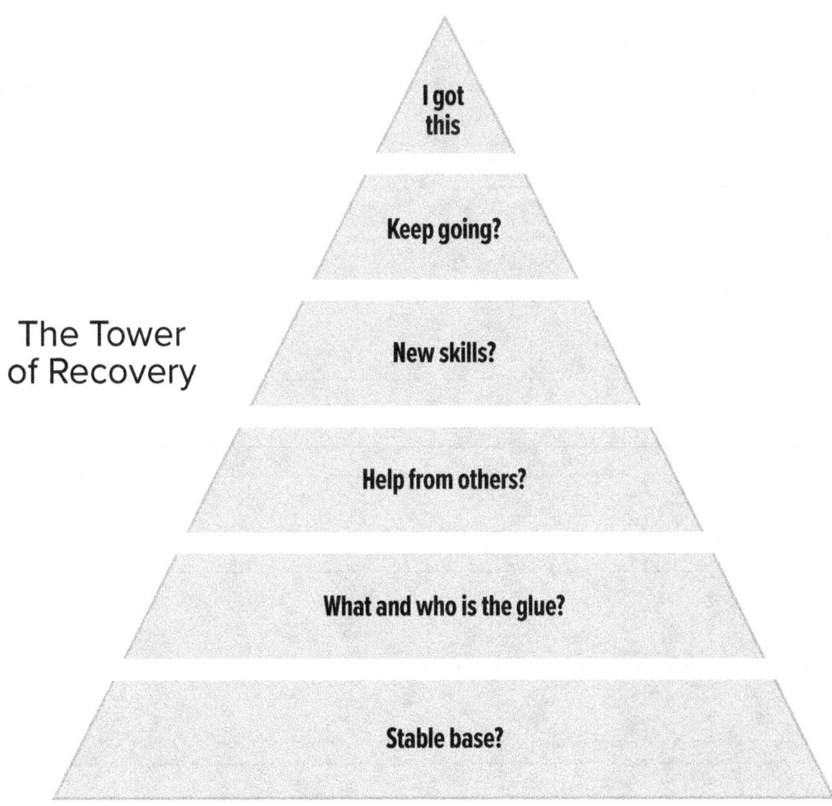

Figure 10

From *School-Based Mental Health Interventions.* © OhioGuidestone. Owners of this book are granted permission to reproduce pages for use with their clients.

Figure 11

How my best friend has supported and helped me:
1.
2.
3.
4.
5.
6.
7.

Figure 12

<table>
<tr><td>Ways in which addiction has betrayed my friendship:</td></tr>
<tr><td>Addiction has asked me to:</td></tr>
<tr><td>Addiction has led to:</td></tr>
<tr><td>Since addiction became my friend I:</td></tr>
<tr><td>Here is what I would like to say to addiction to alter our relationship:</td></tr>
</table>

Figure 13

Figure 14

The thing that will help me prioritize sobriety and recovery is:

Check box when you engaged in the thing that prioritized sobriety and recovery.

MON	TUE	WED	THU	FRI	SAT	SUN
☐	☐	☐	☐	☐	☐	☐

Figure 15

My superhero-like quality is:

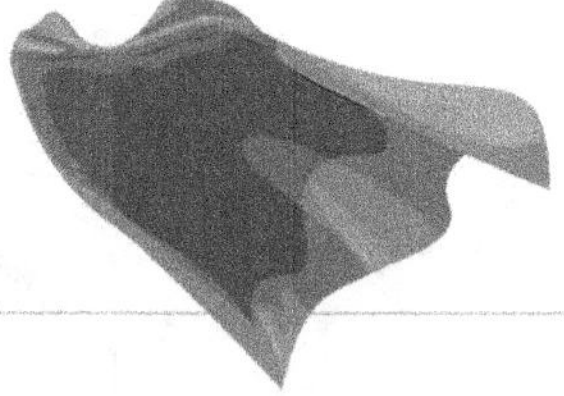

My superhero-like action is:

How I can use this quality and this action to help myself when in danger of using substances:

Figure 16

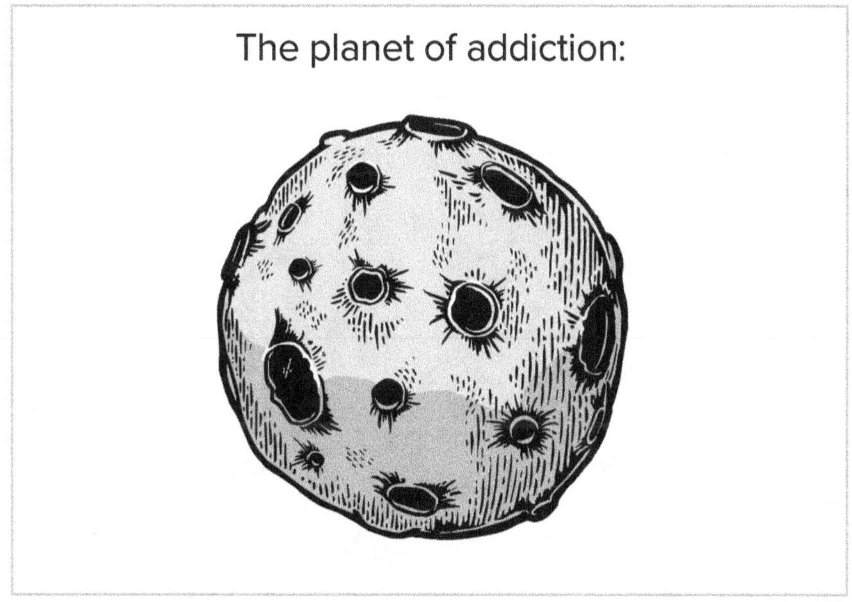

Figure 17

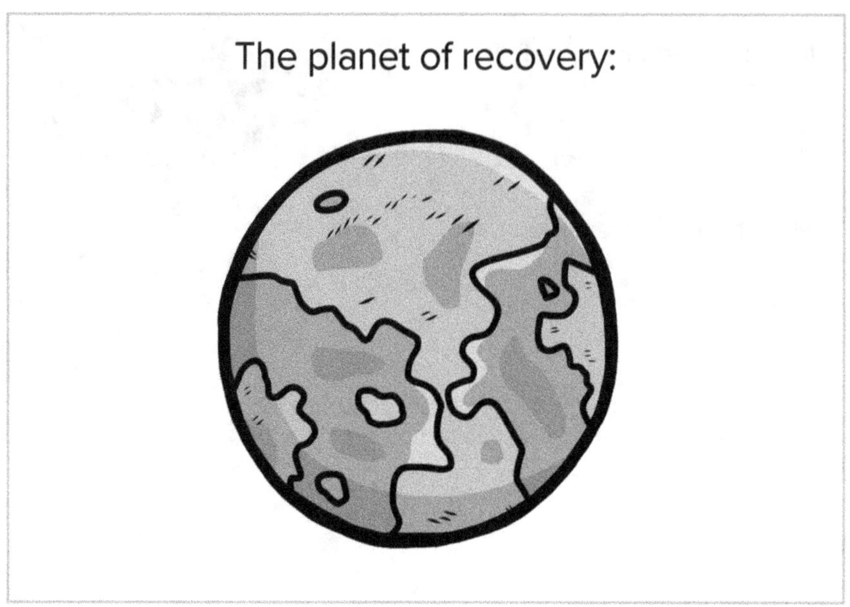

Figure 18

Ways in which I can begin to tear down the wall:

1. ____

2. ____

3. _______________________________________

Figure 19

Figure 20

This week I will: ___________________________________
(insert one of the following: see, hear, speak, trust, feel)

when I am with: ___________________________________
(insert person)

Here is how it went:

Figure 21

Positive qualities about myself that can't be seen at first glance:

1. ____

2. ____

3. ____

4. ____

5. ____

Figure 22

Read letter to myself:	Completed?	Read letter to a friend/family member:	Completed?
How did I feel when I read the letter to myself?			
What feedback did I get when I read the letter to a family member/friend?			

Figure 23

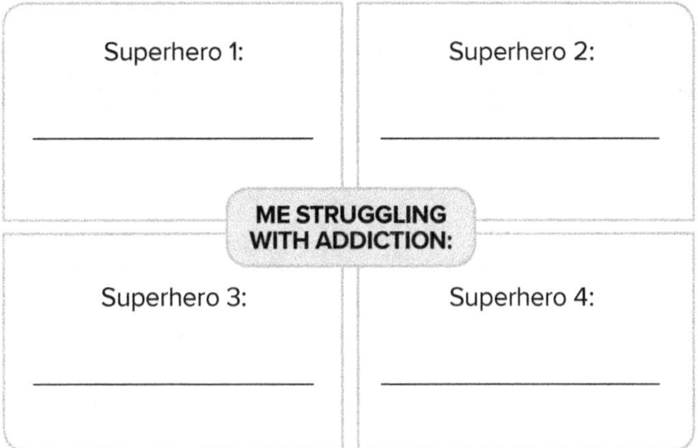

Figure 24

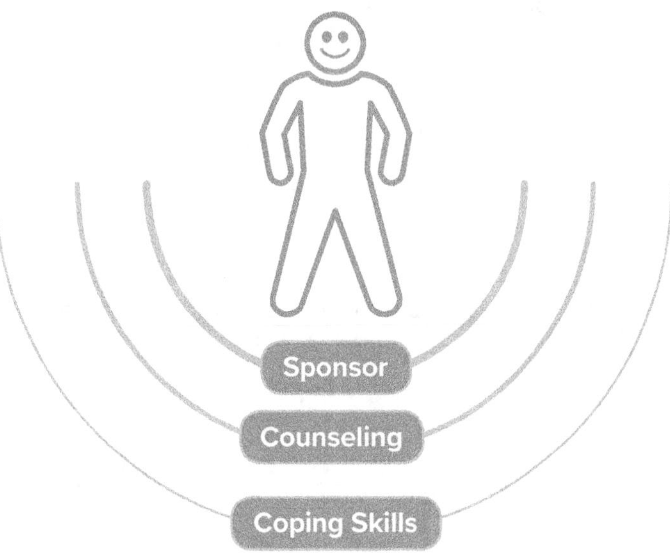

Figure 25

My Safety Net Needs More:

1. ____

2. ____

3. ____

Figure 26

If I were the higher power watching my own process of
addiction and recovery, here is what I would say to myself:

If I were the higher power, here is how I would protect
those struggling with addiction and those in recovery:

Figure 27

Bliss Box Tracking			
Item used:	**Date:**	**Result?**	**New ideas:**

Figure 28

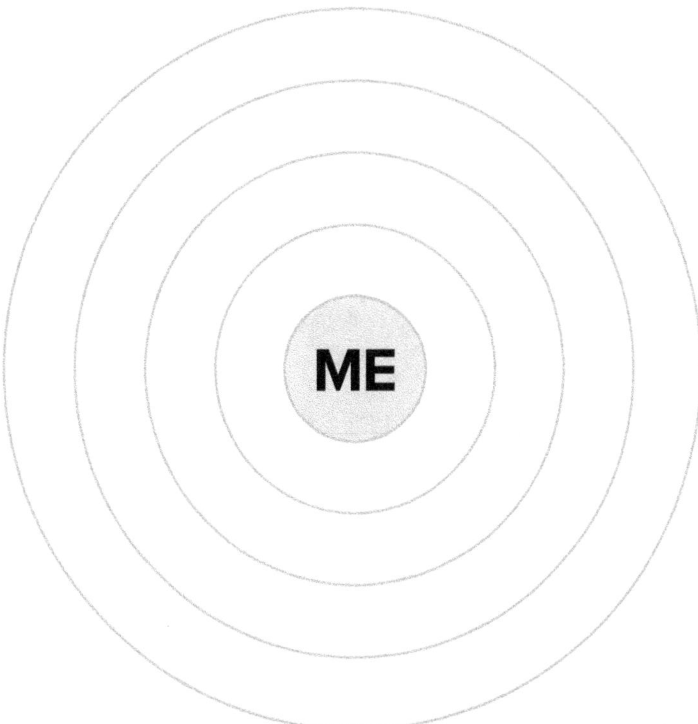

Before my addiction.

Figure 29

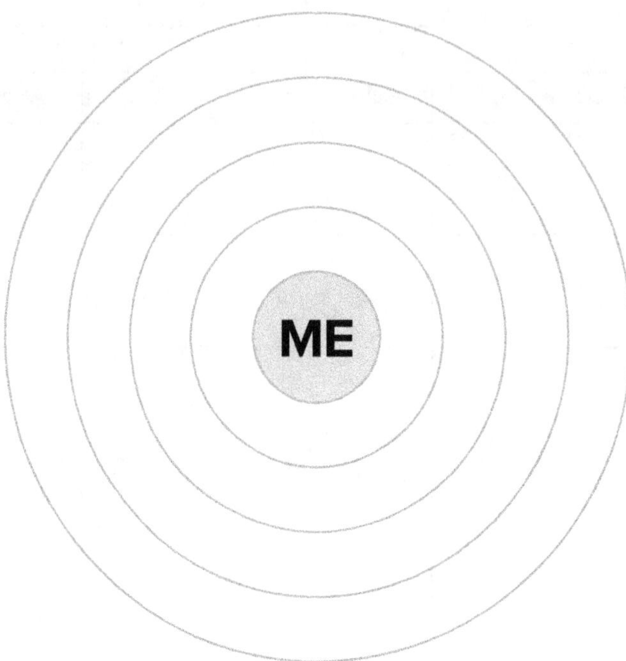

During my addiction.

Figure 30

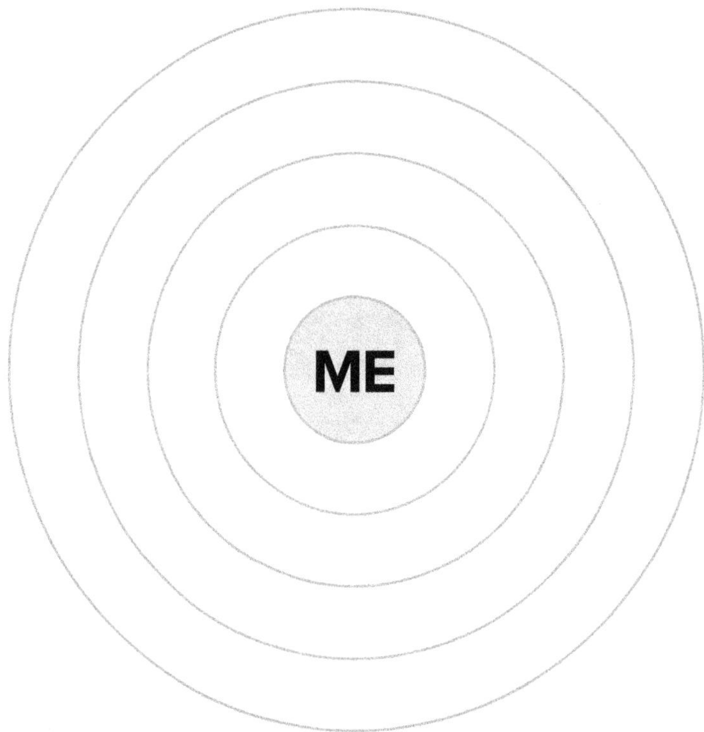

In my recovery.

Figure 31

The person I want in my recovery circle is:

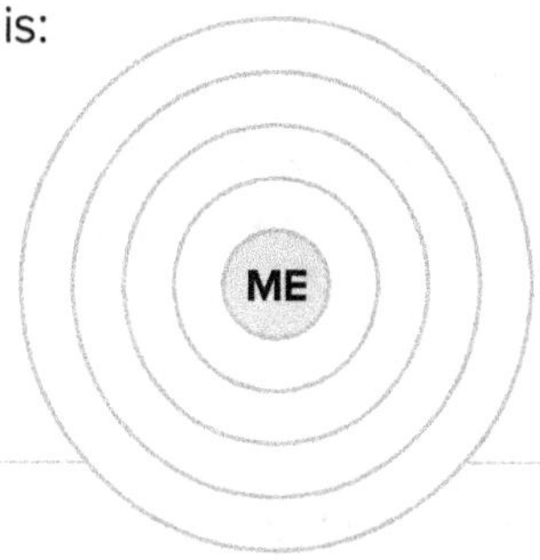

I am going to take this step to connect with this person:

I completed the step above: ☐

Figure 32

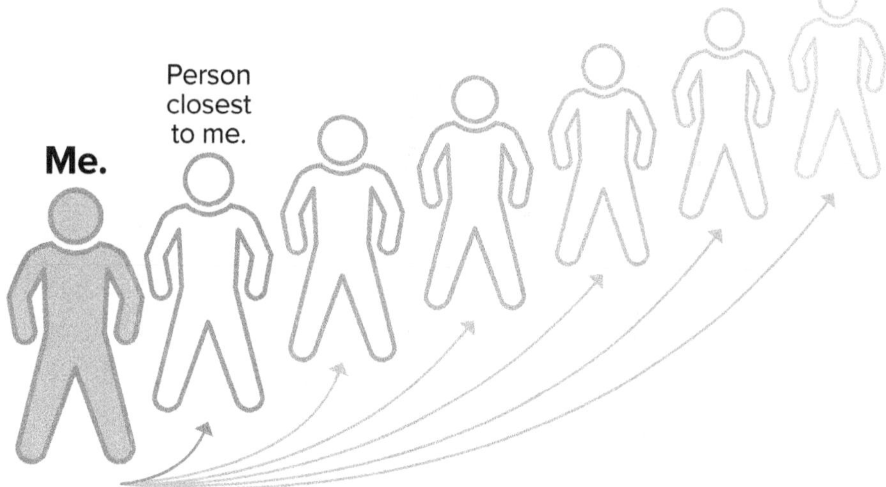

Figure 33

How the future has changed for me
because I am in recovery:

How the future has changed for those close to me
because I am in recovery:

Figure 34

Figure 35

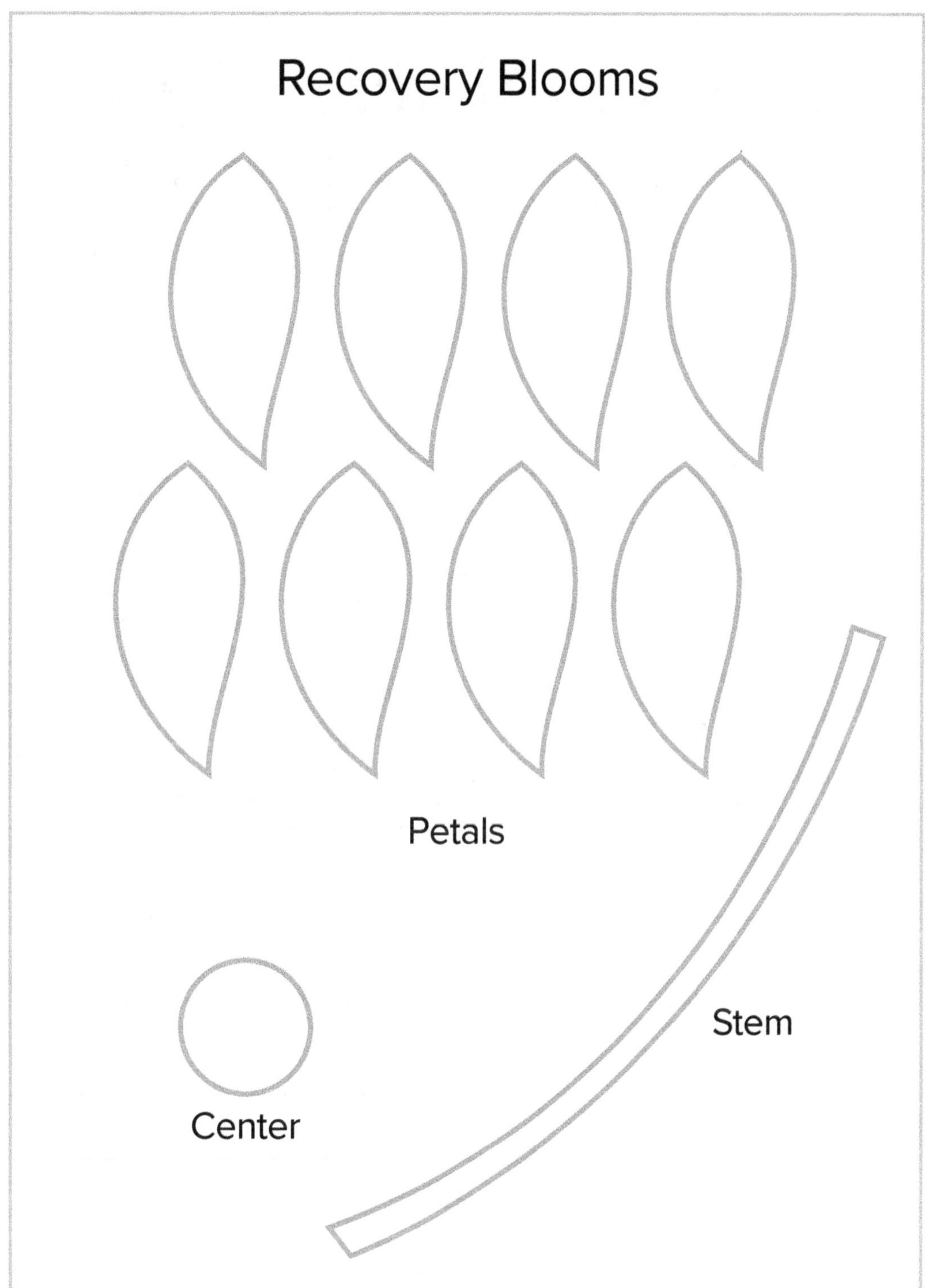

Figure 36

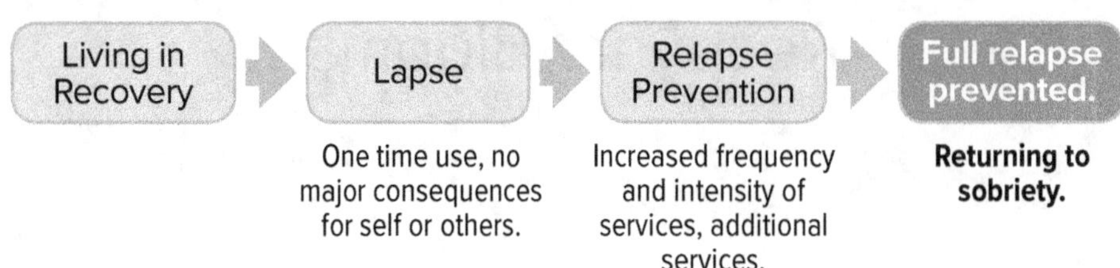

Figure 37

Factors that can contribute to relapse:	Things I can do to address these factors:
Social:	
Emotional:	
Physical:	
Environmental:	
Behavioral:	
General Triggers:	

Figure 39

Planet of Recovery

Figure 40

The ideal planet of recovery has:

1. _______________________________________

2. _______________________________________

3. _______________________________________

4. _______________________________________

5. _______________________________________

Figure 41

Here is a prayer I have said to my higher power/a cry for help I have sent into the world when my addiction got me in trouble:

Here is a prayer/cry for help I need to say now/a request for support that I need to send into the world:

Figure 42

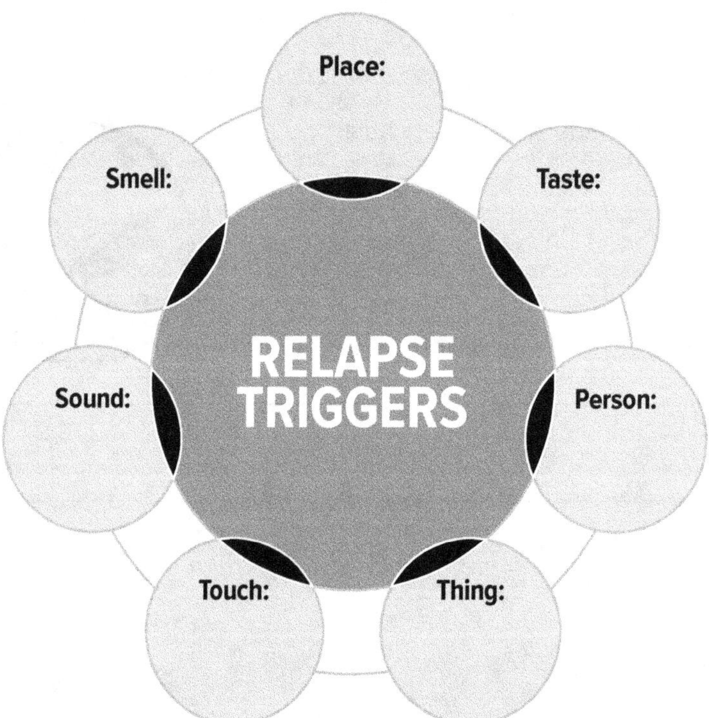

Figure 43

The Book of Faces
Instapost and the Like.

Drug-related posts:

Figure 44

The Book of Faces
Instapost and the Like.

Things I need to do to make my social
media accounts sobriety-building:

1. ____

2. ____

3. ____

4. ____

5. ____

Figure 45

Shelter name:	Shelter phone number and address:	Outcome of call:

Figure 46

Food bank/resource name:	Phone number and address:	Outcome of call:

Figure 48

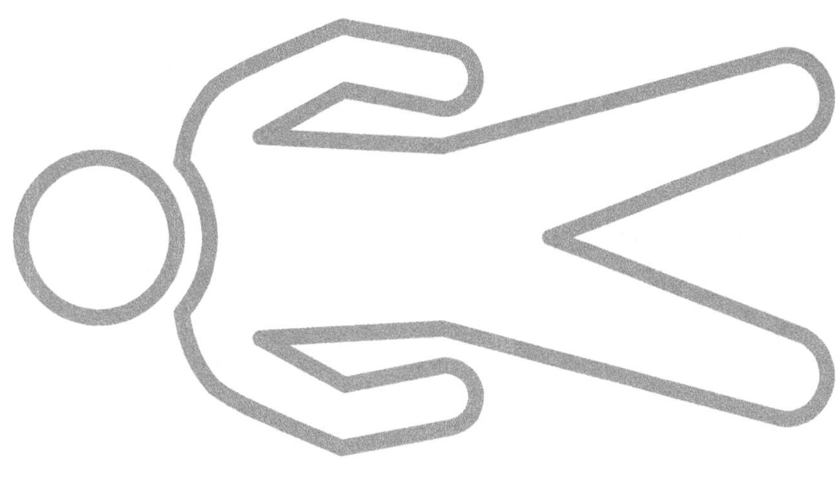

Figure 50

Hi, my name is _________________________________ .

I have not seen a doctor in _______________________

and I am experiencing the following medical issues:

____

____

____

When is your next available appointment?

Figure 51

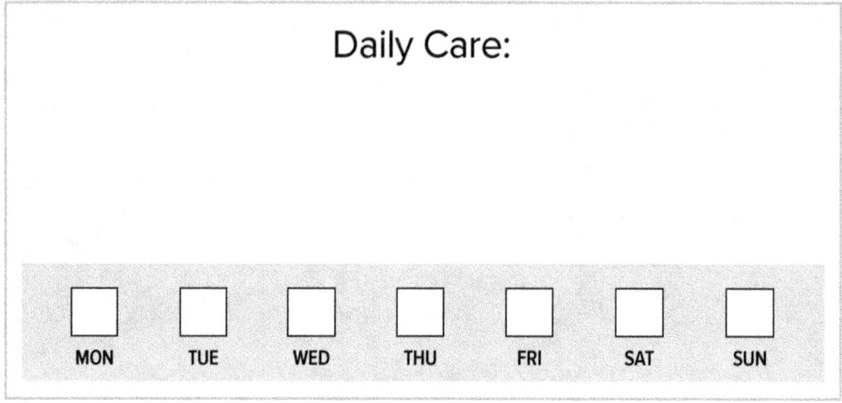

Figure 52

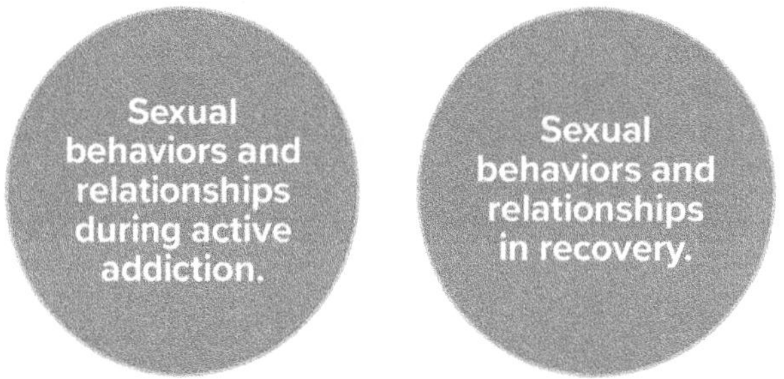

Figure 53

My Sober Days	
Daily Routine: Time and Place	**What I will be doing:**
Early Morning:	
Morning:	
Lunch:	
Afternoon:	
Dinner:	
Early Evening:	
Late evening:	

Figure 54

Things your client can SEE:				
Posters	Pictures	DVDs	Music Videos	Games

Things your client can HEAR:			
CDs			

Things your client can TOUCH:			
Paraphernalia			

Things your client can SMELL:			
Incense	Substances-Alcohol	Clothing	Ashes

Other things that are around:			
Cell Phone #s	Substances-Alcohol	Clothing	Inhalants-Related

Figure 55

Things your client can SEE:	Action plan:

Things your client can HEAR:	Action plan:

Things your client can TOUCH:	Action plan:

Things your client can SMELL:	Action plan:

Other cues:	Action plan:

Figure 56

Income	Expenses

Figure 57
From *School-Based Mental Health Interventions*. © OhioGuidestone. Owners of this book are granted permission to reproduce pages for use with their clients.

Sponsor needs to be:	Reason sponsor needs to be that way:

Figure 58

From *School-Based Mental Health Interventions*. © OhioGuidestone. Owners of this book are granted permission to reproduce pages for use with their clients.

My sponsor should:	Check if yes:

Figure 59

Reason why I am reluctant to go to a meeting:	What could make me less reluctant?	Plan for overcoming reluctance:

Figure 60

What I am looking for in a meeting:	Why I am looking for this:	Is expectation realistic?

Figure 61

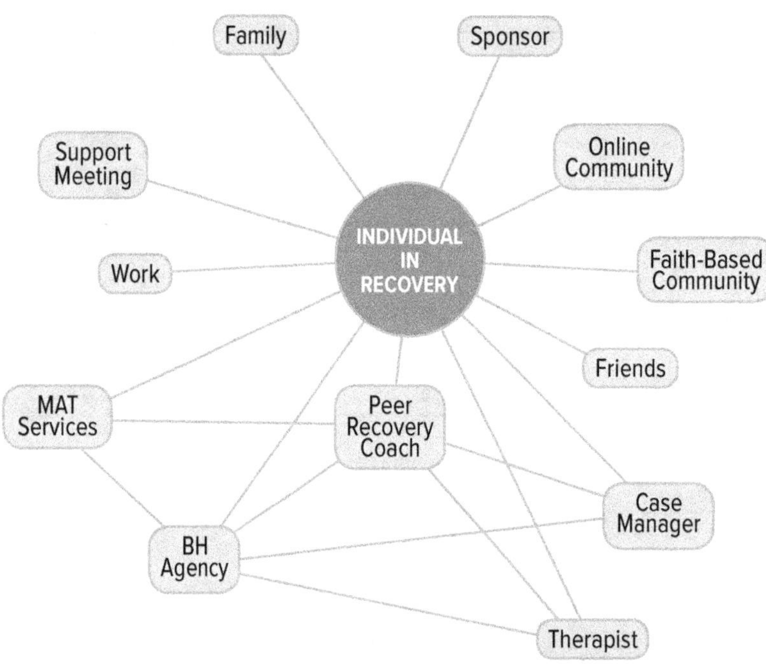

Figure 62

Person most likely to help me stay sober:	1.
	2.
	3.
Place most likely to contribute to my sobriety:	
Activity most likely to contribute to my sobriety:	
Thing most likely to contribute to my sobriety:	
Other things:	

Figure 63

My Sober Hour:

1. Call _________________________________ . Talk with _________________________________ for 15 minutes and/ or make plans to meet up at my designated sober place.

2. Engage in sobriety-embracing activity with my designated person for at least 30 minutes.

3. Show my sobriety-enhancing item _____________ to my designated person. Explain how it enhances my sobriety.

4. Repeat this hourly as needed. If my safe, sober, and supportive friend cannot stay with me for the second hour, plan together who will be there with me. Remember: It's harder to use when a safe and sober person is next to me.

Figure 64

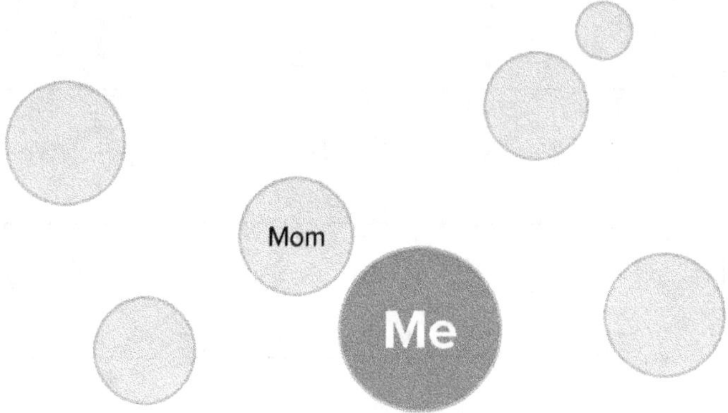

Figure 65

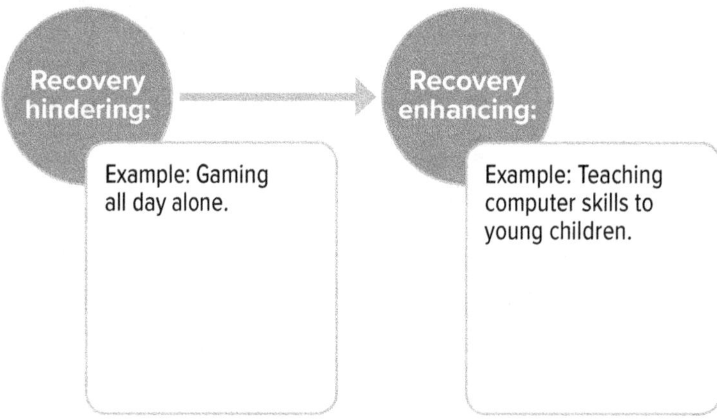

Figure 66

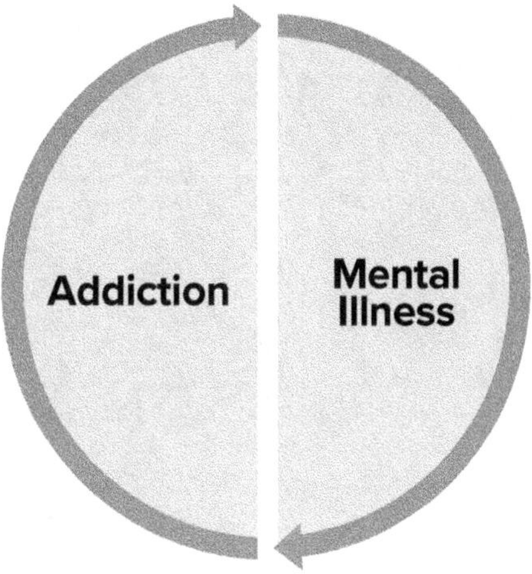

Figure 67

Figure 68